Ride Smarter!

Coralie Smyth

Half Halt Press, Inc.

Boonsboro, Maryland

Ride Smarter!

© 2003 Coralie Smyth

Published in the United States of America by

Half Halt Press, Inc.
P.O. Box 67
Boonsboro, MD 21713
www.halfhaltpress.com

Cover design by Design Point Studio, Epping, NH
Cover photos by Helen Peppe

Library of Congress Cataloging-in-Publication Data

Smyth, Coralie, 1941-
  Ride smarter! / Coralie Smyth.
    p. cm.
  ISBN 0-939481-65-0
  1. Horsemanship--Psychological aspects. I. Title.

SF309.S63 2003
798.2--dc22

Table of Contents

How to Overcome Fear
Body Language
How Important is Position?

Emotions-Causes or Effects?
The Inner Rider
Skills of the Smart Inner Rider

Analyze
Organize
Prioritize
Learning to Say No
Value Quality Time

Horse Psychology
How Do Horses Learn?
The Thighbone's Connected to the Hipbone
Lameness
Conformation
Feeding and Nutrition
Recognizing Signs of Physical Condition
Recognizing Signs of Work

Getting from Klutz to Competent

INTRODUCTION

There is nothing either good or bad, but thinking makes it so.
—Shakespeare

If you are a competitive rider in any of the equestrian sports, you will always strive to be better than you were last time you rode. Whether you are doing dressage, endurance, jumping, reining, hunting, eventing or driving, that need to be better is always there. But the desire to improve won't make you into a top rider—champions are different, but not in the way you might think.

The elite rider is not a superman. He does nothing which the average rider can't do. He has nothing which the average rider doesn't have. His achievements are not based on any unusual intelligence or ability. It's not in his genetic makeup. It's a skill that can be learned—he is an ordinary person. But what is different is his attitude. He thinks differently. And because he thinks differently, he acts differently.

If this is so then it must follow that anyone can become a winner, so long as he thinks and acts the way winners think and act.

Anyone Can Ride Well

Many riders and instructors are still using a 19th-century Model of riding—practicing movements over and over again, riding boring figures ad nauseam, forcing themselves, trying harder, etc. It doesn't have to be like that.

Betty Edwards, author of *Drawing on the Right Side of the Brain* (J.P. Tarcher. 1999), contends that anyone can draw—it only depends on how they look at things. She says "Drawing is a skill that can be learned by every normal person with average eyesight and average eye-hand coordination." Jo Estill, a noted voice researcher and teacher in the United States, has proven that being able to sing isn't an inborn ability! She says, "everyone has a voice, it is just a question of how we use it" and is certain that every one of us has a singer hidden away inside us. Michael Dale, at the Sydney Conservatorium of Music runs workshops titled "Anyone Can Sing." Michael believes everyone can sing. He says it's a birthright and a way of bringing joy into people's lives.

Through the work of people such as these it is being discovered that what we have been taught regarding abilities and learning is not necessarily true, and that if we throw out those beliefs, we can achieve things we never thought possible! Now that educators have a better understanding of how people learn (without tension, by understanding, through doing, with positive reinforcement and by using concepts), we can apply these new techniques to riding and, therefore, progress much faster than ever before.

Unlike other sports, riding doesn't depend on strength, speed or physical conformation. It is a combined body/mind process, and most people have the potential to be a top rider because skills are learned. The mechanics of sitting trot, rising trot, balance, etc. are acquired through practice. The smart rider, however, will learn faster and easier by using his or her mind.

2

What Affects Our Ability to be Skillful?

The things that interfere with our ability to learn are irrational thoughts, non-understanding, negative emotions, fear, lack of confidence, limiting beliefs, etc. And what are all these things? They are all mind things. They are things you can learn to control and change. The things that help us to learn are confidence, persistence, positive outlook, empowering beliefs. These are also mind things.

When we can accept that it is our mind that stops us from riding well and that when we do ride well it is also because of our mind, it becomes very clear that our minds are the controlling force behind the quality of our riding.

So What is Smart Riding?

Smart riding is when you are able to utilize every resource—your mind, body, emotions, knowledge and your horse—as effectively as possible in order to progress very quickly and correctly. Using the mind effectively is the most important aspect of smart riding as it controls everything else. Smart riders improve much faster than others, because of the combination of advanced learning methods and modern training techniques.

You can learn the physical skills of how to ride and you can learn the mental skills. When you learn and use both types of skills, you will be a good rider. When you can additionally utilize emotional control, you will be a better rider.

In order to be a smart rider you also will have a comprehensive knowledge of the basics, understand how to get the best from your horse and manage your time effectively.

Smart riders progress much faster than others because of the combination of advanced learning methods and modern training techniques.

Chapter 1

MIND THINGS

If you think you can or can't, you're right.

—Henry Ford

Because beliefs are not necessarily true, we can choose what we want to believe. Unlike children, who accept what they are told, we are able to discriminate and choose what it is that we want to believe in. While we do have to have core beliefs that are fairly fixed and important to us, we can also be selective about our beliefs in certain areas of our lives.

Naturally, if we can choose our beliefs, we should choose ones that will help us and be constructive for us.

A good way to find out the most useful beliefs is to take an inventory of your present beliefs about riding. Take a moment to answer these questions:

1. *Why do you ride?*

2. *What are your strengths and potentials?*

3. *How do you feel about your horse?*

Let's analyze some possible answers:

1. There are many reasons for riding, but if your answer doesn't include a word like "fun" or "enjoyment" or "pleasure," then maybe you should think again about why you ride.

2. Did this take a long time to work out? Was it hard to acknowledge that you actually do have some strengths and potential? Knowing the qualities that you have is essential to achieving your goals and is much more constructive than concentrating on your weaknesses.

3. Some riders feel that the horse is an animal to be ridden and whose purpose is to help you get to where you want to be. Others feel that their horse is their best friend or part of the family. Whichever category your answer falls into, your attitude towards your horse is vital to fast progress.

If you constantly blame your horse or abuse him, you will find that this attitude will affect everything you do with the horse. If you don't have respect for your partner, you will tend to ignore the messages and communications your horse tries to give you. You won't have a good partnership, and you won't progress quickly.

Now think about:

♦ *How would you act if you were an elite rider?*

♦ *What stops you from acting as if you were a top rider?*

Elite riders are focused, confident, disciplined, determined, dedicated. There is no reason why you can't also have the same qualities as an elite rider. They didn't become focused and disciplined when they became elite. On the contrary, they became elite because they were focused, confident, disciplined, determined and dedicated—all the qualities you can choose to have.

Be Flexible in Your Thinking

A foolish consistency is the hobgoblin of small minds.
—Ralph Waldo Emerson

At a weekend clinic given by a top level instructor, a rider was having trouble going with the horse's movement in the canter and was coming out of the saddle with each stride. The instructor told him to sit down but the rider obviously didn't understand exactly what was meant and didn't alter what he was doing. So the instructor told him again in a loud voice, "sit down." Still no change from the rider. Then the instructor yelled really loudly "Sit Down!" Of course this also had no effect. The instructor didn't have the flexibility to change her advice once she could see that the original command wasn't understood.

In the end, the rider didn't learn anything and, even worse, was labeled as stupid! The instructor would have communicated much more effectively if, when the rider didn't sit down, she had realized that he didn't understand what that meant or how to do it and then explained to him how to keep in contact with the saddle.

Many riders act the same way with their horses. If we pull on the reins and nothing much happens, we pull harder. If the horse refuses a fence, we hit him. If the horse balks at going into a trailer, we punish him. Are these thoughtful, logical actions that are designed to help the situation, or are they our emotional reactions to something we haven't taken the effort to understand?

Instead of using stronger actions, try doing something else. Whenever a horse resists, it is a statement about what you are doing, not about what the horse is doing. It is a very clear message that now is the time for you to do something different and preferably softer.

Holding tight to beliefs means we don't have to think. All we have to do is check the situation with our belief on the matter, and the answer is immediately apparent. However, the best horsepeople in the world are those who have open minds, are always ready to listen to new ideas and are willing to try new methods.

One of the most experienced horse breakers in Australia is Harry Meyer, who is over 70 years old and has seen and done it all. He goes to watch others giving demonstrations or clinics because he feels he might learn something. He still breaks horses (he doesn't ride them much now because he broke a leg a few years ago), and his attitude is that if one thing doesn't work, try something different. He never gets upset, and he produces the best broke horses within a week.

His flexibility and range of choices are very powerful tools.

Many of the things we believe in are true only because we choose to believe they are. There is not necessarily any relationship between what we believe and the truth. The important thing here is that we choose our beliefs-therefore it makes sense to choose the beliefs that are going to be of the most help to us, not those which constantly get in our way.

Most riding beliefs are limiting beliefs—they are negative statements about not being able to do something, and they weaken you. For example: "I'm too old to start riding" or "I'm not the right build for jumping" or "That horse can't do dressage."

Each of these statements is a belief which immediately limits the rider and puts everything into a negative frame of reference. It is much more powerful to have constructive beliefs which strengthen you and allow you to expand your horizons.

Nobody is better than you are, and all sound horses are capable of doing most things.

Don't let others define your capabilities. Never let anyone tell you you're too old, too young, too lazy or too anything to accomplish what you want.

Remember: An expert is merely a person who knows all the reasons why you can't do something. Don't allow yourself to accept limitations set by others.

A university professor wanted to learn about Zen, a Japanese style of Buddhism. The Japanese Zen master could see that the professor was not so much interested in learning about Zen as he was interested in impressing the master with his own opinions and knowledge. The master listened patiently and finally suggested they have tea. The master poured his visitor's cup full and then kept on pouring. The professor watched the cup overflowing until he could no longer restrain himself and said, "The cup is overfull—no more will go in!" "Like this cup," the master said, "you are full of your own opinions and speculations. How can I show you Zen unless you first empty your cup?"

Empty your mind of old habits and beliefs so you will be open to new learning.

Conquer Limiting Beliefs

Change Tense

Instead of making limiting statements in the present tense, put them in the past tense. This stops them from being part of you now and allows you to progress and become stronger.

For example, change "Sitting trot is hard to do," into "Sitting trot used to be hard, but I'm improving." Change "I am clumsy" into "Sometimes I used to be clumsy. Now I'm getting better."

Transform Key Words

Recognize that sometimes we say things in order to make it easier for us to cope. Most limiting belief statements connected with riding start with "I can't...," "You'll never...," or "The horse won't...." In the long run, these excuses end up being limiting beliefs and we accept them as being true. Try changing these negative words into those that are more honest and helpful.

It's *difficult* for me to ...	becomes	It's a *challenge* for me to ...
I *hope* that ...	becomes	I *know* that ...
If I ..., then	becomes	*When* I..., then
I'm going to *try to* ...	becomes	I'm *going to* ...
I *can't* ...	becomes	I *won't* ...
That's the way I am.	becomes	I've *chosen* to be this way.

Now is the time to start recognizing these statements and stop listening to them, whether they are being said by you or by someone else.

Make Affirmations

Just repeating affirmative things will very soon turn your negative thinking around. Choose one of these affirmations, and say it once in the morning and once at night for three days, and you will find that it becomes true!

"I am totally in control of my emotions."
"I am strong and powerful."
"I can do anything I want."
"I am a good person."
"I am proud of what I have done."

One of the most limiting beliefs is "I don't have the ability to be a top rider." If you think about this for just a minute, you will realize that this is an illogical and defeatist statement—and not a smart one.

A number of top riders and coaches were once asked to define what riding "ability" is. Not one could explain it! In fact, there is no special riding ability, even though many people would have you think so. Yes, some people seem to learn faster than others, and some seem to use less energy than others. But these are really skills they have learned, not inborn abilities.

Unlike most other types of sports competitors, riders do not need to have high athletic abilities of speed or power. We need balance, coordination, flexibility, posture and control—all of which we either have or can learn.

Most sports require the athlete to be either fast or strong. Neither applies to horse riders. In some sports like weight lifting, the athlete who has a certain type of build will outperform another—not so with riding. It isn't necessary to have the ideal build or even an expensive horse with magic paces to be successful.

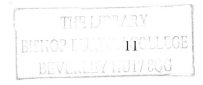

11

There are countless examples of excellent riders who are short, fat or old, and horses who are unfashionable, too old or too small who have made it to the top. None of these has any special ability, but they all have the right attitude!

Always Achieve

There is no such thing as failure. Failure is merely an opinion that a given act wasn't done satisfactorily. Failure isn't a measure of success. In fact, failure isn't anything. In life it isn't what you lose that counts, it's what you gain.

Regard mistakes not as failure, but as a small part of success. It is essential to make mistakes because they are learning experiences. It is, however, unfortunate to make the same mistake twice, and to make the same mistake three times is the beginning of a habit.

There are *some* certainties. Naturally, some things are absolute, such as that horses move away from unpleasant things like pain or intermittent pressure, and respond well to kindness. These are not beliefs but observations made over thousands of years that have been found to be true. It is necessary to be able to differentiate between facts and beliefs so that we don't unthinkingly accept beliefs that may be incorrect.

The Need To Achieve Or The Need To Avoid Failure?

Most people have one or other of these needs, and this need will govern the way they approach things. The person with a need to achieve will relish the challenge of doing something that has some risk or uncertainty about it. On the other hand, the person with a need to avoid failure will usually be more conservative in his or her approach, and will not want to take any chances at all. If you understand what your particular need is, you will be able to motivate yourself better.

12

For example, if you have a need to avoid failure, choose very easy things to do. Make things easy for yourself by breaking them down into very small steps. Each time you accomplish one of these steps and don't fail, you will be more inclined to move on to the next one.

If you have a need to achieve, then set goals for yourself that have some challenge to them. Resist setting goals that are really difficult because you might not achieve them, and that would be demotivating. However, a goal that is a little confronting will be more inviting for you than one you know you can reach without any effort.

You Can't Buy It!

When a goal is associated with some form of emotion, the motivation to achieve that goal becomes strong. If a rider has a very emotional reason for achieving a particular aim, his motivation will be very strong and he probably will achieve his goal.

For example, if a rider desperately wants to jump a big log in order impress his girlfriend, then he would probably do it because his motivation was strong. If a rider feels he needs to prove that he is better than someone he dislikes, the strength of his motivation will provide the necessary determination to do it.

It has been found that, contrary to what might be expected, riders are not very motivated by rewards like material things (e.g., "If you do the whole test without stopping, I'll buy you a new CD.") However, they get really excited by achieving their riding goals, and this motivates them to greater things. Achievement becomes its own reward with riders.

There is no better reward for a show jumper than jumping a height not done before or overcoming a particularly spooky fence. To complete a cross country course in time gives the rider a great high that is impossible to get from a ribbon or even a medal. Performing a dressage test well will motivate any rider to achieve more. Riding in complete harmony with your horse happens infrequently and will motivate you to strive for it again and again.

Climbing the Ladder

Motivation can also come from being aware of your ever-changing perception of the equestrian world and looking forward to the next phase. There are a number of recognizable steps in most sports, and they apply to horse riding quite well.

1. Starting Out
No special gear or clothing is used, there are no conscious goals except to have fun and stay on. Then the rider becomes aware that there is more, finds an instructor and starts to become dependent on them

2. Gaining Knowledge
The rider starts learning theory and skills, finding out about top riders and horses, participating in local events and paying more attention to the appearance of self and horse.

3. Becoming Involved
The social aspects of riding become important—joining a club, assisting in the organization of events, enjoying making friends in riding, discussing mutual interests or problems, learning about state and national levels and developing an ambition to become a good rider.

4. Achievement & Recognition
Riding takes a greater proportion of time, thought and energy. The instructor is less dominating; the rider starts coaching beginners themselves. He performs well at competitions, becoming accepted by peers and building confidence in himself.

5. Knowing

This stage involves realizing that you can do what you want and that you are getting close to your potential. These steps relate closely to the famous *Hierarchy of Needs* formulated by the psychologist A.H. Maslow. Maslow's model is built on these premises:

♦   *People are motivated by a desire to satisfy various needs.*

♦   *These needs are arranged in sequence: the lower ones must be satisfied before the higher ones.*

The figure below shows Maslow's *Hierarchy of Needs* and how closely it can be adapted and applied to riding. When applied to riding, we can see that, for example, a rider will not be concerned with winning a three-day event (esteem) if he is anxious about his ability to stay on (survival). Until a rider is able to control his horse, he won't be anxious to join a club or compete. Likewise, there is no point in learning to jump if the rider is terrified of falling off—the lower order need of control must be satisfied before the higher one of competence.

Maslow's Theory of Motivation   Riding Theory of Motivation

Maslow's Hierarchy of Needs and the *"Riding Hierarchy of Needs."*

We struggle against a lot of things (fear, hunger, poverty, etc), but we also strive *for* things—to grow, to improve and to become more capable. We are constantly trying to improve the quality of our experience.

Rider's Block

Have you ever experienced the confusing predicament of having to force yourself to ride? Did you wonder why it was that something you enjoy so much was avoided so strongly?

Possibly one of the main factors is exactly that—it is something we enjoy, therefore it has to come low on the list of our priorities. We feel guilty if we don't attend to our responsibilities first, and then to our own enjoyment last.

Plateaus

Every now and then riders reach a plateau, where progress seems to slow down or stop completely. It seems to happen to most people—they are conscientious and ride regularly, and then, for no apparent reason, they find it very hard to make themselves ride. If this happens, you shouldn't force yourself to keep going, but give yourself a break instead. Wait until you are really motivated and enthusiastic again. The only reason for riding is because we enjoy doing it.

Finding the motivation again might involve looking into your life outside riding. Do you feel guilty about devoting a lot of attention and/or time to yourself and your horse? Or maybe you have lost the drive you had before. Another theory says that reaching a plateau means that you need the time to absorb what you have recently been learning.

Validation

As human beings we strive to improve, to grow and to increase our capabilities. Not doing these things contributes to low self-esteem, dissatisfaction and frustration. Riding is an activity which is a recreation and, as well, one where we can improve our skill level. It can also be one of the best forms of therapy and rejuvenation. There are many other real benefits as well—constant learning, discipline, control, raising self-esteem and achieving—all those things that are important to us as humans.

Every person needs to have time and space to him or herself, and the more pressured you are, the more important riding should be for you as a means of alleviating pressure and promoting relaxation.

Management

If you want to be an elite rider, you have to ride consistently, rarely having more than one day off. If you are not as determined as that, that's fine—there is no rule that says you must be a top rider and ride every day.

But if you are ambitious to achieve things, then you must ride nearly every day. This means that you have to make time to ride and organize your other activities to fit in.

Work out when you are going to ride. Schedule a definite time, and work other responsibilities in around that. Don't try and handle all of your obligations first and then fit in riding later if you have some time and energy left over—you never will.

Energize

If you still have difficulty persuading yourself to ride, reflect on how you will feel when you have finished—revitalized, more relaxed, happy and more skilled. Remind yourself of your goals and your determination.

The frequency of your riding depends on the strength of your motivation. If your motivation is strong, you will find ways of achieving your goals, even if it means riding at 5:00 in the morning!

Dreams with Deadlines

When you know your destination, be prepared to make the trip. If you want to be a top rider, it is essential to have clear long-term and short-term goals. The accomplishment of these goals is the key to success and to the development of self-concept—knowing who you are and what your riding ability is. Dressage tests and jumping levels are invaluable for this, and help to simplify the process of goal-setting.

How to Set Good Goals

You can control how you actually ride, but you can't control the external product of winning. Therefore if your goal were to be to win, you would often be disappointed. If you set your goals well and are sufficiently motivated, then you will achieve them. So it is very important to know how to set your goals.

There is no point in aiming for the highest level in the shortest time if that is not feasible—you may fail, and consequently lose motivation, maybe even give up. So aim for an achievable level in a sensible time frame.

♦   **Make sure your goals are achievable.**
Set goals you believe can be achieved but also stimulate you to stretch your abilities. Unattainable goals aren't goals, they are fantasies.

♦   **Make your goals specific.**
Your goal should not be "to ride better," which is very broad. However, a goal such as "to make my hands still" is a goal you can easily concentrate on.

18

♦   **Set a time frame.**
A goal doesn't become a goal until you have a deadline for accomplishment. Target times increase your motivation and commitment. As you meet these dates you will feel the satisfaction and pride that comes with meaningful progress.

♦   **Work out the method for achieving each goal.**
Break down each goal into small, easy steps, then work on each step individually. Sometimes it makes more sense to work out the method first and then the time frame. Many times, however, you have the time frame already set for you, for example your next schooling session, or the next event.

♦   **Do it.**
Remember that action is the key to achievement. Failure to achieve goals leads to negative emotional responses such as depression, frustration, anger and demotivation. So it follows that we should always aim to achieve a goal. This is why it is so important to use small steps so you will succeed every time.

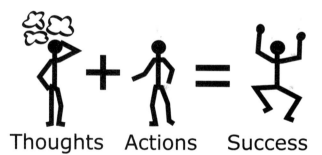

Thoughts   Actions   Success

Success come from thought **plus** action

Short-Term and Long-Term Goals

Riding goals are often already in place for you. For example, if you are riding dressage, your long-term goal may be to ride Grand Prix. Your short-term goals could be to ride the next level test, to learn the movements necessary for the next level, etc. If you are show jumper, your long-term goal could be to compete successfully at A-rated shows; a short-term goal could be to have your horse going calmly.

Being aware of these predetermined goals in an informal way is helpful, but if you are very ambitious you will be doing some serious goal-setting. This involves not only setting the goals, but working out the method of achieving them and planning the time frame needed. These last two are as important as actually selecting the goals and are probably the ones most ignored by riders.

There are many different types of goals—short-term, long-term, performance, schooling and progress goals are just some of them. For now, this list can be reduced to just short-term and long-term goals.

The amount of effort we expend in pursuing our goals depends heavily on their perceived importance to us. We all tire quickly when our energies are directed toward goals we don't care about.

On the other hand, we may devote tremendous effort in the pursuit of goals in which we really believe. Usually we can gauge the strength of our motivation by the amount of effort we are willing to expend in pursuing a given goal; stronger motivation leads to more energetic and persistent behavior and gives a better chance of achieving goals. In general, success tends to reinforce our efforts, while failure tends to have the opposite effect.

Long-term goals consist of a number of short-term goals, and short-term goals consist of many small steps, or chunks. When these are worked out and put on paper, we can see exactly what has to be done in order to get where we want to go. It also reassures us that our goals are possible.

Having to reduce each goal to its smallest steps also gives us a good guide for our training—we can see that each step is easy, and therefore the whole process is achievable. Then we also know how long it will take to get where we are going. This is a great help for motivation.

Short-Term Goals

All training sessions must have short-term goals to be effective. Remember, they must be achievable and specific. Also, you must know what steps you will have to go through (the method) in order to achieve your goal. The closer in time your goal is, the easier it should be. If you are riding tomorrow, then your goal should be a very simple one. When you achieve this, then the next goal, say, for the day after tomorrow, also becomes easy.

You might decide that tomorrow you will work on simple changes. But your goal must be achievable, so it is not smart to have as a short-term goal such as "learn simple changes." You might not make it, and then you will be set back in your program and lose a few days or maybe a week. It's much better to "chunk down" and aim for an achievable goal and succeed—first work on walk-to-canter transitions.

This is the method part of goal-setting—working out the steps necessary for achieving the goal and then starting with the first one. As long as the steps are simple and easy, you won't get into trouble.

The following page shows a possible short-term goal setup for simple changes:

Long-Term Goals

Your long term goal might be to ride Grand Prix dressage. This aim will never be real until you put a time frame on it. This can't be an arbitrary choice; it must

GOAL	TIME FRAME
Simple Changes	Within 2 Weeks
CHUNKING DOWN	
Revise Counter Canter	1 session
Canter-walk transitions	3 sessions
Walk-canter transitions	3 sessions
Canter figure-eights with simple changes through walk	4 sessions
Simple lead changes through X, on the diagonal	2 sessions

involve working out how long it will take you to achieve the intermediate goals of each level, and what you have to do for each one.

Many dressage teachers insist on spending one year on each level, which would mean that progressing from Training or First Level to Grand Prix would take eight years. This happens to be about the time that most riders take for the journey, but that is merely a self-fulfilling prophecy. Many horse and rider combinations have done this in much shorter time, without taking short cuts or ignoring the basics. In fact, if you were to set a time frame of six months per level, and work out a realistic method for achieving that, then it would happen. The limiting factors in dressage are the knowledge and determination of the rider, and the horse's fitness.

To illustrate this point, let's say you are working at First Level with an instructor. You have a good understanding of the basics, and would like to be ready to compete at Second Level within three months. These basics would include having the horse on the bit and in self-carriage, bending, transitions and lateral work. You will soon start working on shoulder-in, simple changes, rein back, travers and counter canter in preparation for Second Level. If you give yourself, say, one week to learn the principles of each one of these, you will need five weeks. Using effective training methods combined with visualization, this is easily accomplished. But of course, Murphy's Law rules, and nothing ever happens that smoothly, so allow an extra week or two over what you have scheduled.

So it could take six or seven weeks to grasp the essentials of Second Level. You still have six weeks to consolidate the movements, rehearse the tests, practice entries, corners and transitions, and to continue to muscle up your horse.

Even though you have devoted two weeks to shoulder-in at the beginning, you will still be doing shoulder-in for three months, in addition to the other new movements. As you need to work less on shoulder in you will spend more time on counter canter, then simple changes, etc. The actual learning part of the program takes only nine weeks, leaving three weeks for learning the test and polishing your riding.

When its put this way, it looks very achievable, doesn't it? Committing your goals, methods and time frames to memory can be hard work, so it is usually better to write it down. Then you can see your progress, watch your self-image and confidence grow, and you become more motivated!

♦   Decide what you want and when. (**Goal, time frame**)

♦   Can you pay the price? (**Method**)

♦   Pay the price. (**Action**)

GOALS	TIME FRAME
Long Term Goal	
Compete at Second Level	3 months
CHUNKING DOWN	
Shoulder-in	2 weeks
Counter canter (+ shoulder-in)	2 weeks
Simple Changes (+shoulder-in, + counter canter)	2 weeks
Travers (= shoulder-in, + counter canter, + simple changes)	2 weeks
Rein back (+ all of the above)	1 week
All of the above	3 weeks

Performance Goals

Remember, there is no failure, only learning.

Performance goals are results-oriented—the ones we want to get when we compete. They need to be controllable and achievable, so aiming to win or to get a high score are not good performance goals. Often this means changing your attitude towards competitive riding. If you compete only to win, you will be doomed to disappointment most of the time.

Failure to achieve performance goals usually results in an extended period of demotivation. Therefore we must ensure that there is no failure. How?

- Don't ride to beat other riders—ride to the best of your ability.
- Compete at a lower level than the one you are currently working in.
- Aim to have more than one goal per event.

Remember, your goals must be controllable. For example, winning is not a good goal because it is out of the control of the rider.

Multiple goals might be

- To be relaxed during the competition, and
- To complete the whole event without stopping.

Some other good competition goals could be

- to be relaxed
- to have a clear round in jumping
- to have still hands
- to ride without resistances

Personal Goals

Personal goals are just for you, and they are all within your control. Positive self-talk is one of the most powerful tools you can use to help achieve personal goals. Some examples are:

"By the end of next week my hands will be quiet and soft."

"Tomorrow I will remain calm at all times, no matter what."

"I will learn the test two weeks before the event."

Training Goals

These are the goals we set for the partnership of ourselves and our horse to be achieved in schooling sessions. If we set these sensibly and take no risks, we will

TIME FRAME	GOAL
Tomorrow	Smooth trot-halt transitions
This weekend	Jump the big log
Next week	Pick up every canter transition

achieve them. For example, you will chunk down these goals into the smallest steps you can think of to ensure that there is no chance of trying something that is out of reach and failing, or of teaching the horse something you didn't want it to know.

Here is a suggestion for chunking down the smooth trot-halt transitions that are in the plan above. It is very easy to chunk down, and once you understand it, you can do it in your head.

CHUNKING DOWN: SMOOTH TROT-HALT TRANSITIONS
1. Trot, half halt, half halt, walk, half halt, halt.
2. Trot, half halt, walk, half halt, halt.
3. Trot towards fence, half halt, half halt, halt at fence.
4. Trot towards fence, half halt, halt before fence

The challenge of jumping the big log is very easy to chunk down—start with jumping something that feels comfortable for you. Then increase the size gradually—so gradually that you can't even tell the difference between one height and the next. You will find that if you start with 18", and then do 20", then 22", after a few times 22" is easy. If the big log is about 24" you will soon be impatient to jump it because it's only a bit higher than the log you jumped a little while ago.

If you tried to jump the big log straight off without chunking, you might have made it, and then again, you might not! It is much better to go a bit slowly and be confident instead of being impatient and taking a risk that could set your training back a couple of weeks.

Once you decide on your goals, put the plan where you will always see it (such as on the refrigerator door, next to a mirror, etc), and check them off as they happen. The more small steps there are, the more checks you will see, and the more checks you see, the more motivated you will become.

The next page gives an example of a plan for a rider's preparation for a one day event.

GOALS	TIME FRAME
LONG TERM PERFORMANCE GOAL	
To compete in the next one day event	2 months
SHORT TERM TRAINING GOALS	
Practice the water jump	Twice a week
Compete twice at Second Level dressage	Within 6 weeks
Get the horse fit	7 weeks
Practice spread jumps	Next 2 weeks
PERSONAL GOALS	
Control inside hand movement	1 week
Ride 6 days a week	8 weeks
Lose 2lbs per week	8 weeks

Chapter 2
IMPROVE WITHOUT SWEATING

The conscious mind is the one that knows the least about what's going on.
—Richard Bandle

Your mind controls your body—if you don't utilize your mind, you are losing 50 percent of your potential. When you use your mind in practice, you can at least double your performance—improve your riding skills faster, decrease tension and nervousness and develop great self-confidence.

Most concentration and competition problems stem from too much brain stimulation. Pressure, nerves, fear, anger and frustration all serve to increase the frequency of our brain waves. Your goal is to be able to slow down your brain wave activity on demand. By diminishing muscle tension you can decrease brain wave frequency, and the more you practice slowing down brain waves, the better you get at it. Breath control training, meditation, yoga, relaxation tapes and exercises can all be used for this purpose.

Visualization trains you to use your mind as well as your body in order to maximize performance.

Right Brain And Left Brain

Visualization is carried out in the brain; it is in the brain that we create images. The brain has two hemispheres which function in different ways. The left brain is analytical, logical, and uses language. It is also very judgemental, assigning blame and guilt wherever it can.

The right brain is image-driven, conceptual and uses emotions——like a jack of all trades that addresses new problems without preconceptions and tries many approaches until it finds one that fits. The right brain doesn't judge; it acknowledges things as they are, without criticizing or condemning.

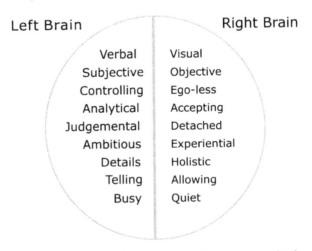

Left Brain	Right Brain
Verbal	Visual
Subjective	Objective
Controlling	Ego-less
Analytical	Accepting
Judgemental	Detached
Ambitious	Experiential
Details	Holistic
Telling	Allowing
Busy	Quiet

The left brain is critical and controlling; the right brain is non-judgemental and image-driven.

The details are perceived by the left, and the whole picture with the right. The left brain notices things taking place in sequence, the right absorbs them simultaneously. The left is the seat of our verbal skills, the right of our visual skills and intuition.

30

The right brain is better at coping with unfamiliar concepts. It contains many long fibers that connect with widely separated regions; the left hemisphere contains shorter fibers that provide richer interconnections within a specific region.

Most people are very good at being left-brained, but as riders we need to encourage more participation of our right brains, especially the nonjudgemental part.

Brain Wave States

The brain operates at different speeds, depending on what it is doing. When you are in a deep sleep it is very slow, and when you are wide awake, problem-solving or stressed, it works much faster.

The main brain wave states are:

* beta: 14-40 cycles per second (normal waking state)
* alpha: 9-14 cps (concentrated attention, relaxed)
* theta 4-8 cps (drowsiness)
* delta: <4 cps (deep sleep)

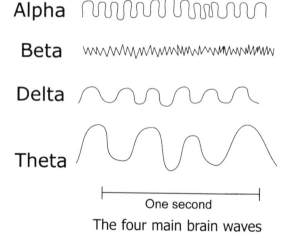

The four main brain waves

Beta

When the brain is aroused and actively engaged in mental activities, it generates beta waves. These beta waves are of relatively low amplitude (a small distance between highs and lows), and are the fastest of the four different brainwaves. The frequency of beta waves ranges from 15 to 40 cycles a second. Beta waves are characteristics of a strongly engaged mind. A person in active conversation would be in beta.

Alpha

Alpha brain waves are slower, and higher in amplitude. Their frequency ranges from nine to 14 cycles per second. A person who takes time out to reflect or meditate is usually in an alpha state.

Alpha brain waves occur naturally as you are falling asleep or day dreaming, and alpha wave activity is at its height as you first wake up. It has been found that as motor skill progresses through stages of learning, alpha rhythms dominate in a corresponding progression from the left to the right hemisphere.

When your brain is in an alpha rhythm state, the right side is most active, while the critical censoring function performed by your left brain is half asleep. Thus when in the alpha state, your self-suggestions can more easily pass through your left hemisphere filter and into your right brain.

As motor skill progresses through stages of learning, alpha rhythms dominate in a corresponding progression from the left to the right hemisphere. Because you are more open to suggestions in the alpha state, new beliefs can be more easily assimilated. Repetition is key and the effects of alpha wave state programming are cumulative.

Theta

The theta brainwaves are typically of even greater amplitude and slower frequency. This frequency range is normally between four and eight cycles per second. A person who begins to daydream is often in a theta brainwave state. A person who is driving on a freeway and discovers that he or she can't recall the last five miles, is often in a theta state-induced process of freeway driving.

Delta

Here the brainwaves are of the greatest amplitude and slowest frequency. They typically centre around a range of one and a half to four cycles per second. They never go down to zero, because that would mean that you were brain dead. But deep, dreamless sleep would take you down to the lowest frequency, typically, two to three cycles a second.

When we get into bed and read for a few minutes before attempting sleep, we are likely to be in low beta. When we put the book down, turn off the lights and close our eyes, our brainwaves will descend from beta, to alpha, to theta and finally, when we fall asleep, to delta.

The alpha and theta states are the most important ones in mental training. When your brain is in alpha, you are conscious but very relaxed, as in the twilight zone between being awake and sleeping. When your brain is in theta, it is functioning slower than alpha. This is the best for learning; neither right brain or left brain is dominant, both are working together. When your brain is in alpha-theta, you learn very fast and you remember very well. This is why we teach our minds and bodies to relax before we do any mental training.

Mental Rehearsal

Traditionally riding has been regarded as a purely physical activity, but it is now becoming clear that greater performance (in anything) will be achieved when mind and body are in harmony with one another and working closely together. There is no substitute for physical training, but visualization will accelerate the training process immensely.

Riding necessarily requires a high degree of awareness, sensitivity and attention. However, training is generally not given in these very important attributes. Training tends to be focused almost always on the body and rarely on the mind.

Riding involves performance with the mind and the body, possibly more than any other sport, because the rider is responsible for the horse as well as himself. Maximum performance can be achieved only when mind and body are in coordination.

Visualization Method

The body must be relaxed and feel warm; the mind must be slowed down and mildly focused. The way we get to this state is as follows:

1. Be somewhere comfortable, such as lying on the floor or in bed, or in the bathtub (make sure you don't go to sleep).

2. Breathe deeply and slowly three times, at the same time smoothing your face and letting the facial tension go.

3. Relax your muscles: start from your feet, and gradually relax each muscle group (legs, pelvic region, stomach,

arms, back, etc). A good way of relaxing muscles is to tense them first, then relax.

4. Tell your mind to operate in the alpha-theta mode, between five and 14 cycles per second.

5. Do the mental work you have planned (mental training, performance visualization, relaxation, confidence raising, etc).

6. Finish the visualization, being aware of how refreshed and good you feel.

Watch yourself performing well.

Visualizing A Performance You Will Be Doing

1. Use the method outlined above. At the fourth step, see yourself on the horse.

2. View yourself warming up.

Feel yourself performing well.

3. See yourself performing well. Be aware of your hands, seat, weight, legs.

4. Do it again, and this time look at your hands. Realize that you are now watching from the inside, and you can feel what you are doing.

Great competitors are invariably great visualizers. They have learned to project themselves into the future and actually see themselves achieving important goals in their minds, long before the actual event.

Self-suggestion and visualization will have the most profound effects if done during slow brain wave frequencies (alpha and theta). Critical, logical, defensive thinking is associated with a very active left hemisphere. For good visualization the rational, logical filters need to be suspended.

During relaxation your brain is more open and receptive to material that might normally be rejected. In normal, more rational states of consciousness, for example, affirmations, might readily be discarded because they often are logically judged to be trivial or irrational.

Visualize yourself overcoming your greatest weakness. If you need to be more in control in competition, vividly imagine yourself being exactly that when riding.

Anger, fear and frustration interfere with concentration because these emotions increase neurological arousal. Depression, sadness and low motivation also interfere, because they decrease neurological activity.

The natural pressures of competition usually increase brain arousal, and relaxation training helps reverse that arousal process. The connection between concentration and neurological arousal explains why relaxation training often leads to significant improvement in concentration skills during competition.

Understand the concentration demands of riding. Riding requires narrow, deep, internal focus. Learn to recognize when you have been concentrating well and when you have not. What does each feel like? What emotions are present?

Learning to reprogram and recondition yourself through combined relaxation and visualization training takes about 10 minutes a day. Naturally, if you do it twice a day you will progress twice as fast. These are acquired skills that will improve with practice.

Focus for Peak Performance

Focus is an integral part of equestrian sport, whether schooling, competing or warming up. Without it, we can't compete consistently and well, and our horses won't learn efficiently. Focus is sort of like concentration, but without the effort. When you focus, you block out the past and the future, and are totally in the present and what you are doing now. Being able to direct and control your attention and that of your horse is more crucially important than any other variable in riding.

In all riding competitions the rider must maintain complete focus all the time. In most other sports, focus can be called on when necessary, and the person can relax occasionally. But riders can't afford to ever lose concentration because they are responsible for the horse's actions as well as their own. This is why preparation is so important for equestrians—if they know as much as possible about the environment, that is one less thing that might distract them when competing.

Eventers and show jumpers should walk the course three or four times; dressage riders should learn the test they have to do. This enables their concentration to be focused on riding well, instead of trying to remember what comes next.

There are two kinds of focus we need to know about—routine and instant.

Routine Focus

Programming for results is the best way of ensuring good performance in a competition and evolves naturally as a result of consistent and repetitive work. The best performers are those riders who are able to keep a clear head under pressure. These people are not necessarily the ones who think or make decisions better under pressure, but they are usually the riders who have done their homework.

It is important to establish in training situations the thought patterns required for competing and to gain practice in making the right decisions away from the pressure of competition. Cool-headedness is a result of rational, logical planning done some considerable time before competition. Without this underlying focus, competing effectively becomes a chance affair.

The key to mental preparation is being able to identify what can and cannot be controlled and realizing that what you focus on can be controlled. Serious riders aim for consistency. This happens with the development of routines. Riders also must be prepared for the unexpected things that will disrupt their routine. For example, if you know it usually takes you one hour to get dressed and warm up your horse at home, when you compete you should allow longer than that because there will certainly be some unexpected interruptions to your routine.

Concentration when you are schooling should consist of thinking only of the present and focusing on a single goal or technique for that time period. Anything that is connected with the past or the future needs to be ignored or pushed away for the time being.

Thinking of the past or the future breaks concentration

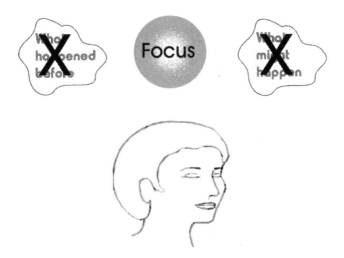

Good focus comes from being totally in the present

When you are schooling your horse at home, make sure you have some sessions where you work as if you were in a competition. If you choose to do a dressage test, ride it all the way through without a break, even if you make a mistake. In the real competition you can't stop and restart the test, so get used to continuing on, no matter what.

Analyze what happens if your mind starts to drift when you are working your horse. Do you lose concentration when there are noises or unexpected sights, such as dogs barking, plastic bags flapping, other horses coming near, someone shouting, etc.? If you allow these things to distract you, your horse will definitely pick up on your reactions and develop an aversion to these things, too. If you remain focused your horse eventually will take his cue from you as the leader and also learn to stay calm.

When you are working with your horse, think only about what is important to you and the horse right at that minute.

Instant Focus

Imagine the impact on your life if you could switch on whatever state you wanted at once—focused, relaxed, in control, happy, etc. This is the bottom line of professionalism in any discipline—being able to perform well at the required moment.

In order to be able to do this at will, you need a trigger—some association with that particular state that we have experienced before. Our minds naturally link experiences—sometimes these associations are very enjoyable, like a favorite piece of music that brings back pleasant memories. Every time you hear that tune it strengthens the association. These triggers or anchors are usually external—a Coca Cola ad that makes us thirsty or the green traffic light that means "go." We can set up internal triggers that are within our control so we can call them up whenever we need them-—this is called instant focus.

We can choose the associations we want to make and associate a physical act with an emotional state. For example, we could choose the emotional state of relaxation and associate that with touching our thumb and forefinger together.

To set up the trigger we would first set up the emotional state of relaxation by deep breathing and relaxing our facial muscles. Then add the trigger (touching the thumb and forefinger). This association then needs to be strengthened by repetition and, eventually, you will be able to relax whenever and wherever you like, merely by touching your thumb and forefinger. And of course, nobody will know that you are doing it.

You probably use anchors already. Do you pat the horse on the neck as a reward? Has this developed into a pat on the neck to calm the horse? Your anchor is the pat on the neck and you linked that from reward to relaxation.

Once the anchors are established, you can use them any time. For example, when you start to get nervous, just breathe deeply twice. If you lose concentration, blink slowly. If you lose confidence, clench your fist.

Invariably, when a competition rider has a mental blank and just loses it, it is because the rider has thought about something else, not concentrating on the task at hand. For example, one competitor rode a 20-meter circle well. She thought about how good it was and congratulated herself. Then she had a mental blank and forgot what was next! Another rider started to worry about a jump coming up and the horse refused the easy one before it ... because the rider lost concentration through anxiety.

This kind of situation can happen at any time. The trick is to be able instantly to re-focus, immediately after you momentarily lose your concentration.

Thinking about the future lets fear beat you.

Thinking about the past lets anger and frustration beat you.

If you fear mistakes, you will make them.

If you fear losing, you will lose.

Mistakes are a necessary part of learning.

Make them fearlessly and aggressively.

Accept what happens and move on.

Relaxed Concentration

Relaxed concentration is one of the most important skills for riders. It is the primary ingredient of the learning process. If we want to know more about something, we need to focus our attention on it that minute—like a laser beam in a dark room.

Trying to concentrate only produces strain and therefore tension. We can't make concentration happen, it occurs only when you allow yourself to become interested in something. If you are not interested, you will quickly lose concentration.

The most important focus for a rider is the horse and how he feels. To control his movements well, you have to be able to feel them, sensing how his muscles and limbs move.

It is the constant thinking activity of the left brain which causes interference with the natural *doing* process of the right brain. Harmony between the two hemispheres exists when the mind is quiet. Only when the mind is still is one's peak performance reached. Quieting the mind means *less thinking*, calculating and judging and *more allowing* things to happen.

It is impossible to truly concentrate when one is anxious or tense. To concentrate, one must be untense and able to focus attention on the present. Thoughts which focus attention on the past or future are distracting and detrimental to attention.

If your mind is in the past reliving previous disasters or triumphs, you will create worry and tension. If your mind is concerned about what might happen in the future, you will create anxiety. Concentration happens when your mind is only in the present.

Chapter 3
LET'S GET PHYSICAL

To increase sensitivity we must reduce the effort.
—Moshe Feldenkrais

In the previous chapter we discussed the conditioning of the mind. However, the mind is not very useful on its own. We need to be able to use our body to the best of its potential.

The Killer of Good Riding

The cause of many riding problems comes from the rider trying too hard, that is, mental tension, which then produces physical tension.

Most riding difficulties can be attributed to tension in the rider. The rest are because of tension in the horse, which is still mostly controlled by the rider. Tension is the killer of good riding and often appears when there is fear. This causes the rider to grip and become unbalanced. When we are unbalanced, we become afraid and tense and so the vicious circle goes on.

Force creates tension and resistance.

Total relaxation is a concept that is often misunderstood and misused. Consider the lower half of the jaw. Most people keep their mouths closed when they are not speaking, eating or doing something else with it. What keeps the lower half of the jaw drawn up against the upper half? Muscle tension. If total relaxation were the correct condition, then the lower jaw would hang down freely and the mouth would remain wide open.

So it follows that if we were totally relaxed while on a horse, we would probably fall off. The ideal state is what I call "untension," where we are using just enough muscles to keep us upright and balanced, but no more than that. Untension is the state we should aim for when riding a horse.

The Tension Cycle

One of the reasons some riders take such a long time to progress is because of fear. Another one is bad teaching methods. When the fear is under control or eradicated, the rider will progress more quickly.

The killer condition of tension can be in the rider and/or in the horse. It can also be transmitted from the rider to the horse and from the horse to the rider.

Productive learning is impossible when there is excess tension in either the rider or the horse—tension in the body creates tension in the brain, which promptly freezes and becomes incapable of absorbing anything.

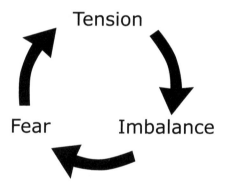

The tension cycle.

When you have any one of these: tension, imbalance, fear, or any combination of them, there exists a situation where learning is not possible because everything is blocked—the brain, the muscles and the body.

The truly elegant rider is untense, confident and balanced.

Causes of Tension

Fear

Horses are very big and very strong animals. Until we learn that we are smarter and can influence their behavior in many ways, we are naturally afraid of them and what they can do. There are a number of types of fear that create tension and stop us from being better riders.

Fear Of Falling Off

One of the most common types of fear—especially for beginners—is the fear of falling off. All of the body's protection mechanisms are used when this fear takes over: abdominal contraction, face tense, head forward, elbows tight, legs gripping, etc. If we can eliminate the fear, we can abolish the tension and restore balance and position.

Fear Of Losing Control

The rider's mouth is often tight, the forearms and wrists are stiff, the back is ramrod straight and the legs are tight on the horse. There is usually an ego factor involved here as well a need to look good, to impress others. This is the rider who feels he has to teach the horse who is the boss.

Fear Of Incompetence

These riders have very high standards for themselves and for their horse. They try for perfection and sometimes even use that as an excuse for not advancing. It is important for them to appear competent. The head bobs, the back is stiff and there is very little softness in their riding. They respond well to moderately hard challenges as they have a need to achieve. However, they will often use force of some kind or another, usually as a punishment.

Fear of Failure

These are the riders who try very hard and, in so doing, make it impossible to achieve their goals. By concentrating intensely on one detail, tension appears, and it becomes impossible to ride softly or loosely. The greater the desire to achieve the goal, the greater the tension, which hinders the achievement of the aim.

While it is possible to reach the desired goal by trying hard, it takes much longer and creates negative reactions in the horse. Delays and resistances are two things which smart riders want to avoid at all costs.

Fear of Success

These people don't want pressure. Achieving a goal means moving on to a new challenge—leaving the present comfort zone and into an unknown and maybe a scary new situation. It also means that there will be new and perhaps greater expectations on the rider. This rider will always find a reason *not* to advance.

Other Causes of Tension

Even though fear is one of the major causes of tension, three others are also important: habit, anger and intense concentration.

Habit

Often a rider will have ridden in a certain way because of fear and then that way has become a habit, even when she isn't afraid any more. But, even though she isn't afraid, the tension is still there.

When a person first learns how to ride, she is afraid and she reacts physically—leaning forward, gripping, rounding her back and pulling hard on the reins. These are all instinctive protection devices and quite natural.

Sometimes, even when the rider becomes more confident, she has by this time developed the habit of holding her body in this protective way. It's not necessary anymore, there is no more fear, but the physical signs are still there.

Anger

Whether it is anger with your horse or anger with yourself, either way it is inevitably destructive when riding. It is always associated with tension and arises from negative emotions like blame or frustration. Anger is counter-productive, ineffective and unacceptable. Often the rider's ego is a contributing cause.

Blaming the horse is an ego thing—a refusal to admit that whatever happens is the rider's responsibility. For example, have you seen anyone mount the horse, start working him and then say that the horse isn't going right, or he's having a bad day? Nine times out of 10 the cause of the horse's behavior is the rider.

Frustration happens when you are unable to achieve your immediate goal, often because you don't understand why things aren't going the way you think they should. For example, perhaps your aim is to have the horse do shoulder-in and it is just not happening. You get frustrated, and your natural reaction is to make your aids more definite so the horse will understand. By doing this, you become more tense, the horse becomes confused and good communication is blocked, so the situation gets worse. In such a case your aims are most likely not realistic. Fix the situation so they can be realistic again. Temporarily revise your aims and make them a little easier. Stronger aids or punishment don't fix the situation; they only make it worse by increasing tension in the horse.

A better solution would be to go back two steps, to where you know the horse understands you and do some easy stuff first. Then gradually progress again, in very small steps, staying relaxed and encouraging.

Before you blame the horse for anything, first make sure that you have been perfect in every way.

Concentration

Often when a rider is concentrating very hard, she will hold her breath. This causes muscular tension, with all the accompanying problems. The answer to this is to visualize first, then do it. Visualize again, then try again.

Signs of Tension

Tension is most obvious in the rider's joints (knees, ankles, wrists, elbows) and the extremities (fingers, head, neck, face). Other places tension appears are the lower back, stomach and shoulders.

The visual signs of tension

When a person is tense or concentrating hard, she forgets to breathe. Because holding the breath is a sign of tension, exhaling will help to decrease the tension. There are some good methods to encourage breathing: try singing, talking about what you are doing, saying the alphabet or counting aloud (the number of footfalls per quarter circle, perhaps). These techniques also encourage the right brain to take over from the left brain.

Whenever there is tension, the rider will not be naturally balanced. She can only stay on the horse through gripping, which, in turn, effects the horse and adds to the fear.

How To Overcome Fear

Breathe

The first step is always to breathe. If you are tense you are probably holding your breath, so exhale loudly. Then consciously relax the legs and body. Because the horse is always attuned to the rider's breathing and tension, this breathing and relaxation is unconsciously transmitted to the horse.

Relax

The body can influence the mind; therefore, to change a mental attitude, try to change the physical attitude first. When a rider is afraid, her shoulders tense, her stomach tightens, her mouth and facial muscles contract. If you change even one of these physical symptoms, you will find your mental attitude has no choice but to change as well.

If your face is tense, your whole body will also be tense. So relax your face by smiling, yawning or singing, and your body will follow the lead and become relaxed too.

Identify the Fear

The first step to reducing or eliminating the fear is identifying the cause of it. Ask yourself: Is the fear rational? Is the cause of the fear under your control? Is it anxiety (fear of what may happen in the future)? Insecurity? The horse? Nerves? Other people? Unpreparedness? The judge? The task to be done? Making a mistake? Losing?

Eliminate the Fear

If the fear is rational and the cause is under your control, then fix it. This might mean going back to an easier movement or a smaller jump, training or retraining the horse, or retreating from a situation which is scaring you or your horse. Don't try to force yourself to do something that you find fearful. Go back to doing what is comfortable and progress in tiny stages.

If the cause of the fear is not under your control, then remove yourself from it—move away or get off. Don't be a hero or get into a battle of wills with the horse. Either action will have a negative result. If the fear is irrational, use some strong self-talk.

Body Language

On the Ground

How we treat the horse on the ground has an effect on how the horse will behave when we are mounted. Horses are herd animals, and they recognize the herd leader. If you can establish that relationship on the ground, your job will be much easier when mounted and it doesn't have to be a battle, either.

Horses are quite subtle about a lot of their behavior and they will recognize similar subtleties in us if we are smart enough to use them. One of the easiest behaviors for us is to restrict the horse's movement. This can happen when we just stand in front of the horse—if he gives way to us, we are the herd leader. Then it can become even more subtle, by merely turning a shoulder toward the horse.

When the horse allows us to do things to him, like putting on gear, leading, grooming, picking up feet, etc., he is acknowledging that the handler is the boss. So when we actually mount the horse, it has already been agreed that we are the boss, and the horse is the follower waiting for our instructions.

The way we touch a horse is also important. Patting him on the face is uncomfortable for the horse and perhaps even painful and yet they accept this from people. Stroking around the face and scratching around the body are activities that are more acceptable—horses do that to each other and they like that.

The way we walk toward a horse will tell the horse very clearly what our intention is. If we are in a hurry to catch the horse in a paddock, we walk differently than if we are just going to spend some time with the horse and feed it some carrots. Horses pick up the difference very quickly. If we walk directly to the front of the horse, this can be considered aggressive. Walking to the side of the neck is more acceptable; walking backward or sideways toward the horse often helps if the horse is very spooky. Basically, if the horse knows we will not cause him pain and we will give him pleasure, he will be happy to see us and to come to us of his own free will.

Mounted

When we are riding, our attitude should always be to *allow*, the horse to do things, while we give it direction or encouragement and help in the way of aids and signals.

Trying to force or make a horse do something is futile and counter-productive. If we have already established who is boss before we mounted (and the fact that we were allowed to mount is indicative of that), then it is unnecessary to belabor the point and create resentment.

Perhaps more importantly, the use of force, fear or violence will stop the horse from thinking—it becomes confused and is unable to comprehend what is happening. There are two possible solutions here: use more force and beat the horse into submission, or use less force, restore calmness and try a different, more intelligent approach.

It is a bit arrogant if we think that we can force the horse to do what we want. The horse is so much stronger than us, we can only achieve what we do because the horse cooperates or because we know how to employ some kind of leverage. It is much cleverer and more effective to set up a situation and then let the horse do it. For example, in teaching a horse to perform a rein back, set up a situation where it will profit the horse to move backward, and will be uncomfortable for him to move forward.

One way to do this is to have unyielding hands so that if the horse tries to move forward, he comes up against the bit that blocks him; if you squeeze with your legs (which usually means move forward), and he can't, wait until he tries to go backward to avoid the blocking hands, then make sure your hands reward him by not blocking any more. In this way, you have set up a situation that has only one way out that is rewarding for the horse—your job is to be patient enough to let him do it in his own time.

Health and Fitness

The more efficient your body is, the better you will feel and the better your results will be. Deep breathing, as well as being a great aid to relaxing and focusing, is also a most effective way to clean out the lymphatic system (the system that helps to protect against infection) and eliminate toxins in the body. So when you breathe deeply to overcome nerves or to start mental training, you are also cleaning out toxins in your system.

When you have no obvious excess weight, you will ride better, look better and feel better. So eat better and exercise more. Your diet should consist of water-rich foods: fruits, vegetables and sprouts. All other kinds will add to the build-up of waste products in the body, instead of helping to keep the system clean. So have at least one salad a day along with your regular meal and eat fruit for snacks.

The best exercise riders can do is aerobic exercise (aerobic means "with oxygen")—moderate exercise sustained over a period of time. Like horseback riding.

The reasons for warming up before exercising are (1) to gradually mobilize the fatty acids into the bloodstream so your system can utilize these instead of blood sugar and (2) to gradually distribute blood to areas that need it rather than immediately diverting it from vital organs like the heart and lungs. This should take about 15 minutes and applies to both people and horses.

Warming down for 10 minutes after exercise is also very important for people as well as horses—walking or other mild exercise is fine. In this way the lactic acid is dispersed from the muscles so cramps and stiffness will be avoided.

How Important is Position?

Why is there so much emphasis on rider position? Surely if you are going to sit on horse, you just sit on it, right? Well, yes, provided you are relaxed, balanced and the horse doesn't move!

Problems arise because sitting on a horse isn't at all like sitting on a chair—a chair isn't scary and it doesn't move, so we can remain relaxed.

On a horse, our first reactions are to hang on with everything possible—hands, legs and seat. Of course, to many trained horses, gripping legs mean "go forward" and pulling back on the reins means "stop." So as soon as we are on the horse we start giving him many conflicting and confusing commands without even realizing it. The horse then reacts in a way we don't expect, so we get more frightened and hang on tighter!

When we learn to relax more on the horse, we then find out that as soon as the horse moves, it upsets our balance and makes our body move around in ways we don't expect. So we try to correct this and in doing so, we over-correct, again confusing the horse and setting up another vicious circle.

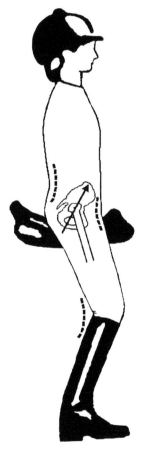

A good position has all the joint angles in a neutral state

And then, when we eventually get accustomed to this strangeness, we find out that if we want to do sitting trot or canter without getting bounced out of the saddle with every stride, then we have to do something a bit more active on our part than just sitting and being relaxed. We have to learn how to absorb the shock and accommodate the movement of the horse.

A good position allows you to be direct and efficient and is one from which you can move in any direction. Therefore, it follows that your joints need to be in neutral—not too open and not too closed. This is the best state to allow the joints to open or close as effectively as possible and with the least amount of tension.

When riding, all good movement is directly involved with the pelvic region. This is where the most powerful muscles of the body are attached and, therefore, the least amount of effort and activity is required to move the upper body in any direction. By the same reasoning, the smaller muscles and extremities, the hands and feet, should move the least, thus ensuring a quiet seat and the smallest upset to the horse.

A good position is not derived from elegance. It is one of balance, from which the rider will be able to control his horse effectively. Elegance then becomes a natural consequence.

How Can We Achieve Good Position?

Most instructions that are given regarding position use a very left-brain method and describe every important aspect in detail. Of course, it is impossible for the rider to remember all of these directions in addition to trying to control the horse and remain relaxed, all at the same time!

It is much easier to take the right-brain approach and feel that you are relaxed. Check out the main joints—lower back, elbows, knees. Be comfortable. Balance on your seat bones. That's it.

Don't worry too much about things like making your shoulder, hip, heel a straight line, or stretching up with your body, down with your legs—that will happen automatically. Don't try hard to do anything. Just let it happen.

Be Loose

If the rider is balanced on the two seat bones, in a state of untension, using no superfluous muscles, she will be in a position to give light and independent aids, in a state of equilibrium so that whatever the horse does the rider will be able to accommodate any unexpected movements.

This has to be a conscious right-brain attitude until it becomes habitual. It is counterproductive to be constantly analyzing each part of your body for faults and then telling that part to change. It's much better to adopt a position of balance and untension and to feel if your position is right.

The Secret of Balance

Balance is the governing factor in security and comes when all joints are supple. It is the natural adjustment of the rider's weight to conform with every movement of the horse.

Your posture and balance while on the horse is dependent on your seat and your untension. All joints should be relaxed and in a position from where they can easily open or close (halfway between both extremes).

1. Your seat bones should be in the deepest part of the saddle, which is very close to the pommel.

2. Your lower back must be slightly concave, so that you are able to easily increase or decrease this curvature as required.

3. Your legs hang down with the knee slightly bent.

There is one other thing to remember with the balanced seat: make sure that your upper body doesn't collapse over your mid-section. Keep your back long but not stiff, slightly behind the vertical.

The three-point seat is advocated by some people. Presumably these points are the two seat bones and the crotch, but when looking at a skeleton, this appears to be an anatomical impossibility. Even if these three points were able to be in contact with the saddle, the pelvis would have to be tipped forward and the lower back would be curved inward to such an extent that there would be no possibility for any further absorption of movement. The rider then would have to rely on muscular tension to stay on the horse.

Others say the three points of contact are the seat bones and the tail bone—this also would also be anatomically impossible for many people and would straighten the lower back, again not allowing absorption of movement.

Stability comes from two factors. The first is internal balance which is largely dependent on the position of the centre of gravity of the rider's body. Sally Swift, in her book *Centered Riding*, says that your center is just below your navel, and in front of your spine. Your center of gravity will be raised if your muscles are tense and will be lowered with muscle relaxation. The stable position lies where the pull of the force of gravity holds the body in a vertical position. When the rider's center of gravity is low, she will then be best able to follow the horse's movement at the trot and canter.

The second factor in stability is where the rider's center of gravity is in relation to the horse's center of gravity. According to Wilhelm Müseler, in his book *Riding Logic*, when the horse has his neck more or less arched, and his head slightly in front of the vertical, his center of gravity lies slightly behind the mid-point of the shoulder blade. When the rider's center of gravity is aligned with the horse's center of gravity, the rider will be in the least displacing point on the horse's back.

Absorption of Shock

The quick, big movements of a horse produce shocks that the rider must absorb. The flexibility of a rider's joints acts as a shock absorber, especially the lower back. The *F.E.I. Dressage Manual*, Article 1917, says, *"Only the rider who understands how to contract and relax his loin muscles at the right moment is able to influence his horse correctly."*

The loins are where the fronts of the thighs join the torso—where there is an angle when you sit. The loins must be supple (untense) enough to allow that angle to open and close. This indicates that the lower back is also supple and thus the whole shock-absorbing mechanism can function correctly.

The stiffness of a joint will affect the rest of the body above the joint. This is especially noticeable when the lower back is stiff—the shock can't be absorbed and continues up the spine until it meets the head, which then (incorrectly) starts to nod.

♦   If the loins aren't supple, the shock isn't absorbed and the rider bounces up and down in the saddle.

♦   If the knee joints are locked, the lower leg sticks out from the horse and aids can't be subtle.

♦   If the ankle joints are stiff with the heel up, the center of gravity is raised, interfering with balance and the rider will feel insecure.

♦   If the elbows are stiff and sticking out from the body, the hands will move up and down, making the bit unsteady in the horse's mouth.

61

When the horse walks and our lower back is supple, the horse moves our pelvic region backwards and forwards, passively opening and closing the angle of the loins. When influencing the horse, the rider has to actively move the pelvic region in order to go with the movement of the horse. The way to do this is to move the seat bones from the back to the front with each stride.

The Iliofemoral ligament

Why is it difficult to open the loin (hip joint) while riding when we do it easily while standing on the ground? Basically because, when we are on the horse, our legs are pushed out away from our hips. In order to compensate for this, we either bring our knees forward, bending our legs to accommodate the curve of the horse's barrel, or we tilt our pelvis forward, increasing the curvature of the lower back, allowing our legs to be more vertical.

Some riders tend to adopt either a chair seat (closed loins, lower back natural) or a crutch seat (open loins, lower back concave) because these seats are more comfortable. But each of these styles is wrong and the correct one is difficult—because of the iliofemoral ligament.

This is one of the strongest ligaments in the body and connects the femur to the pelvis. Its function is to limit motion and provide stability. It limits abduction (the thigh moving outward) and lateral rotation (the thigh moving backward).

It's because of this ligament that riders tend to adopt an incorrect seat. The rider will either tip the pelvis back (chair seat) or tip it forward (crutch seat) so that the iliofemoral ligament isn't stressed.

In the balanced seat, the two most important areas are the loins and the lower back. These work together to maintain rider balance and to effectively influence the horse. When one is flexed, the other is extended and vice versa. If the rider adopts a seat that puts either of these

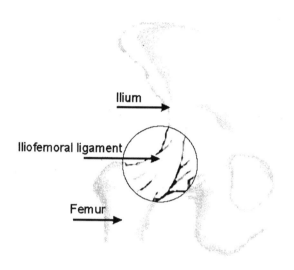

Ilium

Iliofemoral ligament

Femur

The ilio-femoral ligament restricts backwards and outward movement of the leg

areas into an extreme position, she will be unbalanced and ineffective, unable to influence the horse with her seat and incapable of absorbing the movement of the horse.

The ideal seat has the lower back and the loins both in a neutral position, so that movement in any direction is easily obtainable. Additionally, concussion is more readily assimilated through the lower back when it is in a neutral state, enabling the rider to stick to the saddle in sitting trot and canter.

The chair seat has a good lower back, but closes the angle of the loins. This makes the rider unbalanced.

The first option, which lets the upper leg go forward, allows the lumbar spine to remian correctly curved and the rider to sit mainly on the seat bones. But, when this happens, the rider sits toward the back of the saddle with her legs forward. This is comfortable but places the rider away from the horse's centre of gravity, which impedes her balance and often necessitates the use of muscle tension in order to stay on.

The crutch seat puts the lower back in an extremely concave position, stopping any pelvic movement.

The other alternative is for the leg to hang down vertically, but then the pelvis tips forward making the lumbar spine increase its curvature. This creates the three-point seat (pubic crest + two seatbones) and will not allow the spine to absorb the movement of the horse, forcing the rider to bounce or nod his head.

The iliofemoral ligament is often shorter in women than in men and the female pelvis is tipped more forward at the top than the male, which can tend to make the correct seat more difficult to achieve for women.

The Balanced Seat

The ideal seat is one that allows the rider to

♦ effectively control and influence the horse
♦ absorb the horse's movement and
♦ maintain balance and stability

The balanced seat has the lower back with a natural curve and the angle of the loins is midway between open and closed.

True balance on a horse can only be achieved by keeping the lumbar spine curved in a normal, natural way by tucking the seat bones under the body—bringing them closer to the front of the saddle and opening up the loin angle. This has the effect of dropping the leg directly under the body, which enables the upper torso to remain vertical and over the horse's center of gravity and for the lumbar spine to retain the proper curvature. However, this needs a fairly supple iliofemoral ligament and many riders find they have to exercise a little bit to get that extra flexibility.

This is the only position that a rider can have that provides balance, accommodation of the horse's movement, the least amount of muscle tension, effective control and influence. Only in this way can the rider be light, balanced and relaxed, with control of the horse through his seat. The horse is not distracted by unnecessary movement and the aids can be clear and unmistakable without using strength.

Stretching exercises on the ground can prove valuable to many riders if they are having difficulty opening the loins when riding: gently swinging the leg backward with the body upright; the legs apart and bent, with pelvic thrusts; leg raising to the side; legs apart, with sideways pelvic swaying, forward and sideways lunging are all helpful.

Lightness and Harmony

Anything that is performed with difficulty, with pain or strain is worthless; you will never enjoy using it. When activity is free of tension and superfluous effort, the resulting relaxation makes for greater sensitivity, which makes for still greater effectiveness in action.

Often riders have the problem that the horse won't move forward until he is kicked many times and very hard. In order to solve this problem we have to make the horse more sensitive and reduce the effort needed to get going. This is done by giving an aid with the lower leg. When the horse does nothing, use a crop behind your calf. This must be done less than one second after the soft aid. As soon as you see that the horse begins to anticipate the signal from the crop and starts to move immediately on the leg signal, stop using the crop. Then you should use an even softer aid and continue to get softer and softer until you only have to think squeeze and the horse will move.

The same technique can be used to halt the horse, getting lighter and lighter with the reins until he will halt merely with a slight pelvic movement from the rider and no reins at all.

It's very important to not pull backward on the reins ever—blocking, or being unyielding, is much more effective while pulling will only cause the horse to pull against you.

Choice Of Movement

Lack of choices makes strain habitual.

For effective movement, the heavy work for a rider to move her body must be shifted to the muscles designed for this purpose. The largest and strongest muscles are connected to the pelvis. As we move away from the center of the body to the limbs, the muscles gradually become smaller. The muscles of the limbs are intended to direct their movements accurately, while the main power of the pelvic muscles is conducted through the bones of the limbs to the point at which it is required to operate.

In a well-organized body, work done by the large muscles is passed on to its final destination through the bones by weaker muscles, but without losing much of its power on the way. Excess tension in the muscles causes the spine to be shortened. Therefore, unnecessary effort shortens the body. In every action in which a degree of difficulty is anticipated, the body is drawn together as a protective device against this difficulty. It is precisely this reinforcement of the body that requires the unnecessary effort and prevents the body from organizing itself correctly for action. This self-protection and superfluous action are expressions of the person's lack of self-confidence.

When the rider is loose her body will automatically adjust to the horse's movements without having to think and reorganize herself. If the rider has to go through many of these left-brain thinking steps, all balance is lost and tension appears.

Energy Transmission

Forces working at an angle to the main path lose energy.

Under ideal conditions, the work done by the body passes through the spine and limbs in as near to a straight line as possible. If the body forms angles to the main line of action, part of the effort made by the pelvic muscles will not reach the point to which it was directed. The more angles and bends there are for energy to go through, the less energy there will be where it is needed.

Action becomes easy to perform and the movement becomes light when the huge muscles in the center of the body do most of the work, and the limbs only direct the bones to the destination of their effort. Good body organization makes it possible too carry out most normal actions without any feeling of effort or strain.

It might be said that good riding is just controlling the horse's energy using our own energy in the most efficient way.

The skeletal structure should counteract the pull of gravity, leaving the muscles free for movement. The nervous system and the frame develop together so the skeleton can hold up the body without expending energy despite the pull of gravity.

If the muscles have to carry out the job of the skeleton, not only do they use energy needlessly, but they are also being prevented from carrying out their main function of changing the position of the body—that is, movement. In poor posture the muscles are doing a part of the job of the bones.

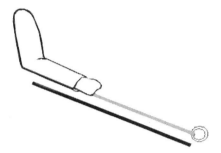

There should be a straight line from the elbow, through
the wrist to the bit.

If the bones and muscles attached to them are rotated, such as in our forearm and wrist, the transmission of energy is interrupted. This is why we keep our thumbs uppermost—this keeps the wrist aligned and forearm bones straight—and have a straight line from elbows to bit, as seen from above as well as from the side. Imagine a very long ruler running from your elbow to the bit. The back of your forearm and wrist will lie along that ruler.

As well, the underneath line of your arm/hand/rein should be straight. Sometimes it happens that the rider bends the wrist down, which takes muscular effort and makes sensitivity impossible.

Turning the lower arm in or out takes muscular effort, which creates tension. Bending the hand outward or inward has the same effect. Keeping the forearm and hand in the best position just also happens to be the most untense position! So don't try hard to make sure everything is correct—just feel that there is no tension.

However, we do have to hold the reins firmly. The horse needs to be able to feel the bit, where it is and what it is communicating. If we ride with "soft" hands, supporting the reins between loose thumbs and forefingers, we are not giving the horse any support or sense of security, we can't feel what is happening and when we need to be firm we will actually bang the horse in the mouth, hurt him, and lose his trust.

Chapter 4
HOW DO YOU FEEL?

A bad rider gets angry. A good rider gets better.
—Coralie Smyth

Feelings are the results of human thoughts and are enormously important. Most of our activities and thoughts elicit feelings, and our feelings mobilize us to respond to various stimuli. However, when we allow feelings to control our actions and thoughts, our riding suffers greatly.

Some emotions are empowering and encourage a rider's talent and skill—drive, confidence and persistence. Other emotions are disempowering and effectively lock out your potential—anxiety, insecurity, worry, fear and confusion.

Often, positive emotions can fire you to reach your peak, but when your excitement takes over, you may begin to be careless and make mistakes. Strong negative feelings will affect a rider physically, creating tension, stiffness and blocking.

Emotions are the energy in life and are stimulated by whatever touches on a person's self-interest and instincts. They are not necessarily an end in themselves, but part of the process toward adjustment or balance.

Emotions—Causes or Effects?

Don't find fault, find a remedy.

Emotions are not bad or good—they are, in fact, like signposts. They provide us with basic information, which helps us to interpret situations. For example, when a rider experiences the emotion of anger, it means she is being blocked or frustrated. The experience of the emotion of happiness can indicate that the rider is functioning well, and in harmony with the horse. Negative emotions such as anger and fear give us information that we need in order to take some kind of action. The positive emotions such as happiness and calmness encourage us to recreate similar, rewarding situations so we can experience them again.

If you are ruled by your emotions, your future is unpredictable. Give total control to your emotions and you give up the power to be your own person. Feelings ought not to set direction. Direction comes from the mind, not the emotions. Emotions are a by-product of living, not the reason for living.

Many people suffer from the delusion that emotions are entirely out of their control: that they're just something that spontaneously occurs in reaction to the events of our lives. In truth, the source of emotions is you. You are the one who creates them, which means that you can feel any way you choose at any moment in time.

- If you look upward, you will feel confident.
- If you smile, you will start to feel happy.
- If you frown, you will begin to feel doubtful, or even angry.
- If you consciously relax the muscles of your face, other body muscles will automatically relax as well.

To make your riding really work, you must make your emotions work for you. If you magnify them and allow them to take over everything then you become incapable of making decisions and your riding becomes controlled by random events.

However, denying emotions (even negative ones) is not the solution. If they are suppressed they will keep on intensifying until you acknowledge the message they are giving you. But you can decide to deal with unwanted emotions at another time or in another way, thereby neutralizing the negative effect on your riding.

Positive Emotions

These are the emotions that make us feel good:

Happiness

Remember that riding is fun. The only valid reason for riding is because we enjoy it. If we don't enjoy it, we're crazy to do it.

Smart riding is therapeutic—you will always feel better after riding than you do before you mount the horse. Smart riding is also very rewarding—you know that you will achieve something every time you ride.

Confidence

Confidence comes from having previously coped with the same or similar problems. If you haven't actually experienced the exact same situation, which often is the case when riding, try one of the following:

♦ Think back to when you handled a similar situation. For example, you might not feel confident about cantering on a horse you haven't ridden before. Recall the feeling of cantering well on your own horse and how you were able to cope with that.

♦ Remind yourself that you have the skills. You know how to use your aids; you know that if you relax, so will your horse.

♦ Remember that you are the one with the control. The horse accepts you as the herd leader and he will try hard to do whatever you want.

♦ Realize you have choices. If you know you have a choice, that is, if it doesn't work one way you can use another method, then your confidence will increase.

Determination

With determination you can accomplish anything. It dictates how you deal with upsets and obstacles. Without it you will always have frustration and disappointment. The rider who wants to achieve things but doesn't have the determination will always be finding excuses—the weather, health, time, gear, etc.

The rider with determination will ride in spite of apparent obstacles. For example, if the weather is very hot, the average rider might say that it is not good to work a horse in such heat, so he takes the day off. The Smart Rider will say, "OK, it's hot, so we'll just work on easy stuff like the walk, rein back and halts."

Determination is always associated with action. There is no point in being very determined if it is only in your mind. You have to actually do something and continue to do it. Even if it is only something small, with determination this small thing will grow.

Determination is also associated with goal-setting. We must have something to aim for before we can use our determination to ensure we get there. However, be careful not to make the goals too challenging, or you will experence the negative emotion of disappointment. Have a major goal (like qualifying for a major show), but also have minor goals, such as overcoming nerves, keeping your horse calm, maintaining concentration or using a lot of preparation.

Negative Emotions

These are the emotions that signal to us that there is a need to change something:

Anger

Anger serves to protect the real self from pain and nerves. It helps overcome fear and makes it easier to regain a sense of control. It is therefore important to know that when you become angry this is a message telling you that you need protection.

For example, when you ride badly it could be because you lost your temper or had a bad day at the office—not necessarily because you are an incompetent rider. Telling yourself you are stupid and unworthy has the effect of reducing expectations and helping to control nerves. Anger that is obvious also lets everyone else know you are not really that bad and that you are aware of the problem.

The emotion of anger lets you know that what you're currently doing is not working, either because of the way you perceive things or because the procedures you are using aren't working. Either your aids are not effective (probably too strong), or they are not the right ones. Then you have to change your approach. Maybe you're being too harsh, or you expect that the horse already knows what you want or how to do it.

Anger signals that you need to change what you're doing.

Anxiety

Anxiety is worrying about the future and is a great producer of tension. As we discussed previously, it is not possible to focus when the mind is concerned with the past or the future. Anxiety is one way for your brain to keep occupied and busy so the solution is to divert the attention of the brain to the present and concentrate on what you are currently doing.

The physical signs of anxiety include the feeling of the stomach tied up in knots, the need for constant adjustments to the position and seat and unnecessary movements of the hands and fingers. To an onlooker, any extraneous movements will indicate anxiety.

Anxiety signals that you need to change your thinking.

Frustration

This happens when we are continuously putting out effort but not getting rewards. This means that your brain believes that you could be doing better than you are—a positive sign.

It also means that the solution to your problem is within range but what you're currently doing isn't working. It's a strong signal for you to become more flexible. Treat it as a learning situation.

Frustration signals that you need to change your approach.

Disappointment

This can be a very destructive emotion if it's not dealt with quickly. It occurs when an expectation you had didn't happen and this makes you feel frustrated, sad or defeated.

Now you have to look at other outcomes, to make them more appropriate for this situation and take action to set and achieve a new goal immediately:

- ◆ Figure out what you can learn from this situation that could help you in the future.
- ◆ Set a new goal that will be easier and just as exciting.
- ◆ Realize that you may be judging too soon, that the situation may not be over yet .
- ◆ Make things a bit easier for yourself and your horse.

Disappointment signals that you need to change your goals or expectations.

In one way or another, the solution to each one of the above negative emotions is change—your way of thinking, your actions, your approach, your focus or your expectations.

Stress

**To love winning is easy;
to love doing the work requires toughness.**

Stress is the environmental stimulus, or signal, which leads to anxiety (mental response) and arousal (physical response).

A moderate amount of stress is beneficial, but when stress gets out of control it becomes a negative force. People who thrive on stress and successfully manage it have the feeling they are in control.

It is this perception of a lack of control which leads to feelings of helplessness and anxiety. When this happens, a person's systems begin to break down and we become more and more self-preoccupied. Then we find that there is a tendency for most people to have self-centered and interfering thoughts and behaviors; the subconscious seems to be working against us. We can't think in a rational way, and our body freezes.

We need to convince ourselves that, in reality, we do have control over the situation. Then we can relax and have control over ourselves and our horse.

77

This convincing can often happen by going back a few steps and remembering what it was like when we did feel in control. Some things we can do include:

♦   Using visualization to see ourselves in control.

♦   Watching someone else ride the horse without a problem.

♦   Analyzing what created the lack of control, and either eliminate that cause or change it.

Stress is the external factor that produces either anxiety or arousal. It isn't always a bad thing and we can train ourselves to be able to handle it and even use it to our benefit. To get emotionally tougher you must get a little stressed often, then recover. Stress is anything that causes energy to be expended; recovery is anything that causes energy to be recaptured.

Stress can be managed if recovery periods are included at the right times.

Physical stress occurs when you move muscles a lot; mental stress when you think, visualize and concentrate a great deal; emotional stress when you feel fear, anger, tiredness, etc. Recovery occurs at the same three levels as well. It often simply means getting rest or changing focus.

Talking can often stimulate emotional recovery, as can writing, painting, movies, music, nonriding exercise and meditation.

Excessive emotional stress leads to physical and mental problems. In order to protect ourselves from the unpleasant consequences of stress, we can become unmotivated, depressed, moody, negative or listless.

Stress Analysis

Where does your main stress come from?
- ❑ parents/spouse
- ❑ instructor
- ❑ friends
- ❑ you
- ❑ your horse

What are the best indicators that you are stressed?
- ❑ bad temper
- ❑ moodiness
- ❑ apathy
- ❑ irritation
- ❑ tension

What are your best recovery mechanisms?
- ❑ riding
- ❑ talking
- ❑ sleeping
- ❑ physical activity
- ❑ music

It's important to be able to recognize when you are getting stressed—to know what our specific symptoms are. Then, because you also know your recovery mechanisms, you can fix the problem quickly without letting it drag on for days.

Under the pressure of competition, we always break at our weakest links. This occurs at every level—physically, mentally and emotionally. When the pressure is on, this is where you will break.

Know what your specific weaknesses are and practice inflicting them on yourself in a noncompetitive situation. Also train yourself in recovery mechanisms that you can use such as breathing, putting the problem in a box until tomorrow, diverting your attention, doing something physically active, looking up, smiling, etc.

To get tougher, focus your training on your weakest links.

Arousal

Arousal is the physical result of stress, which often comes from mental and emotional sources. In general, it has been found that for every competitive activity, an individual needs to be aroused to a level above his normal resting state. If the level is too low, the competitor may not expend the energy necessary to attain his goals. At the opposite end, exceedingly high levels of activation tend to impair both physical and psychological functioning because of the accompanying tension.

Riders need an increase in their arousal level, but only to a very small degree—just enough to ensure that the brain is working well and they are focused. Any more arousal (tension) and they will get nervous, make mistakes, go blank and worst of all, try hard.

The fact that high arousal levels are not conducive to beginners or to anyone learning a new skill has important implications. During the introduction of new material, arousal levels should be held a low level, both for the rider and the horse. Sessions should be interesting, well organized and enjoyable. Competitions should be used for motivational purposes with great caution, since the increased arousal may retard learning and/or performance.

Additionally, each performer's self-perception of competence may also affect the interaction of arousal and performance level. If a rider's self-assessment of her skills or preparation is low, arousal may be increased.

It also has been shown that high levels of arousal affect balance and precision tasks more negatively than skills requiring strength or power. So those skills requiring pure strength, such as weightlifting, or pure speed, such as the 100-meter sprint should be performed under higher arousal levels.

Riding and other precision sports such as golf and archery require low arousal levels. Both horse and rider should aim to remain as calm as possible.

The Importance of Control

Control over our own levels of arousal is important and can be done by using various techniques such as relaxation methods, visualization, self-talk, etc. However, by themselves, the techniques are useless. The initial step required before using any of the techniques is one of self-monitoring—identifying the symptoms associated with excessive levels of arousal.

Riders can be taught to find out which of their body systems reacts most for them under pressure and then become in tune with how minor variations within this system influence performance. The next stage is to develop the skills that allow them to modify their arousal level. Self-regulation skills can be learned, just like any other skills.

All anxiety is accompanied by physical tension; when physical tension is gone, emotional tension is released. If you become aware of bouncing in the saddle, nodding your head, pulling on the reins, leaning forward, hunching your shoulders, gritting your teeth or pushing your chin forward, these are signals that there is tension in those particular areas which is resulting in stiffness or blocking. Once you can recognize these symptoms, it becomes possible to fix them.

The next step is to establish where the tension is and learn how to eliminate it.

Anxiety Control Strategies

As we discussed previously, anxiety is the mental tension produced by stress of some kind. It is usually regarded as worrying about the future and what might or might not happen then. However, knowing what it is doesn't give us the means to control or eliminate it. There are quite a few different ways of coping with this kind of stress.

Mental Training

The Australian Institute of Sport says that the last thing learned is the first thing that breaks down under pressure. Usually the new skill will work until it is tested, at which time the rider will probably fall back on the older, more comfortable way of doing things.

Mental training is invaluable for fixing a new skill and thus reducing pressure. It uses visualization techniques, just like mental rehearsal or relaxation. In mental training the rider sees and feels themselves performing the new action correctly, first as if they are on the horse and then as if they are on the ground watching themselves riding.

Relaxation Techniques

Top riders seem to be able to perform with a minimal amount of energy being expended. The aim of general relaxation training is to increase sensitivity, which will assist the rider to significantly lower her muscular tension under the stress of competition. Riders need to learn how to control excess arousal fluctuations, or they will be incapable of handling the pressure of high-level competition.

Relaxation always begins with conscious breathing, slow and deep, then visualizing and feeling the muscles as being warm and heavy. Breathing out loudly will be heard and recognized by the horse and it also serves to relax many muscles in your body.

Counting breaths up to 10 is a great way to distract your mind from tension-building thoughts. Make the breaths very deep and as soon as you have inhaled into your diaphragm as much as possible, exhale and count that as one breath.

Looking upwards is another confidence builder. For example, people who are about to walk over hot coals are always advised to look up just before they start as this gives them an inner feeling of toughness. This can also help riders to relax just before competitions.

Smiling relaxes the muscles in your face, which then transfers to other muscles in your body. It's not hard to find a reason to smile or laugh-—just thinking about how ridiculous it is to get uptight about a silly competition should usually do it!

Overpreparation

Being prepared is good, but being overprepared is better. One of the biggest mistakes riders make is to compete when they are not ready for that level. This can do a lot of damage to the subsequent attitudes of the rider and the horse if that performance is not satisfactory. Conversely, if the partnership is well prepared, they will be confident and have no fear of competing in the future.

The more times a rider has competed, the greater his chances of coping with the stresses of competition. However, this doesn't necessarily mean that inexperienced riders or horses will not cope on their first appearance. If they have done a lot of high-quality practice, they will be well prepared for the pressures of an upcoming competition.

Again, visualization can help a rider to become mentally prepared as long as it is very positive, utilizing feelings and images that are confident, correct and competent.

Attitude Modification

The problems of tightening the muscles, lacking control, being inflexible, etc., are similar in that they are all caused by our way of observing, interpreting and reacting to a particular situation. The key to solving such problems involves a change of attitude.

Attitudes are habits of mind. As with repeated movements that become second nature, we form patterns of thought and feelings about situations and events, which eventually become part of us. Some of these attitudes are necessary, but when they are fixed instead of flexible, then we have problems.

The first thing we have to do is to be able to recognize that our attitude needs changing. Go back in time to when you were just pleasure riding:

- Was it fun?
- Did you look forward to it?
- Did you act nicely to your horse?

Now that riding is a bit more serious:

- Is it still fun?
- Do you look forward to working your horse, or do you have to make yourself ride?
- How do you treat your horse? Do you ever blame him for things that don't go right?

Your answers to these questions will give you a guide to your attitude and if it needs changing.

Why should your attitude be any different now that you are more serious about your riding? Basically the only change is that now you feel you have to ride. It has become an obligation. However, it doesn't have to be like that. You can decide to change your attitude back to what it used to be—just like that!

You can decide that riding still is fun and that now it's even better because you also achieve something each time you ride. You can look forward to your time with your horse as being valuable and something you rearrange your day around, instead of fitting it in if you have time.

And, of course, your new attitude means that you will never blame your horse when things go wrong, because you are the one in control—the decision-maker.

Just for today,
I will be a soft rider.
I will control my emotions.
I will smile when I make a mistake.
I will be satisfied with what I have done.

The Inner Rider

Have you noticed how often you talk to yourself when you're learning something new or competing? Most riders are talking to themselves most of the time. "Sit up straight." "Keep your hands down." "Be careful." "You could have done that better." The instructions and exhortations never stop.

These inner conversations have been analyzed by Timothy Gallwey, a writer, teacher and sport psychologist, in his books on inner games (specifically on tennis and golf). His rationale also applies very well to riders and is of crucial importance to those who want to ride smarter.

The Two Selves

Gallwey theorizes that we all have two inner selves: one who seems to give the instructions and the other who seems to perform the actions. Then the first self returns with an evaluation of the action.

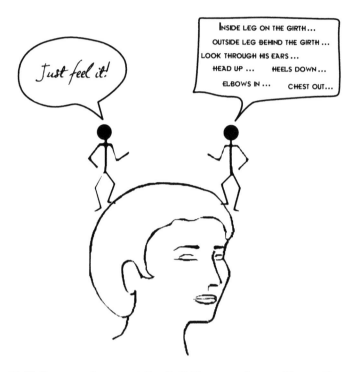

Self One analyzes while Self Two performs the actions

Self One does all the talking, while Self Two just does things. Self Two absorbs and remembers everything that happens to us without trying or moralizing. Self One analyzes and judges constantly, always concerned with values and worthiness. Self Two accepts things as they are, very much like a horse. Your horse doesn't analyze events or try to be a better horse than others: he might try to be faster or more beautiful, but goodness isn't part of his life. When Self Two does things, Self One is always around, criticizing and evaluating them. This evaluation is the cause of many of our riding problems.

The key to better riding lies in improving the relationship between the conscious, analyzing egotist and the unconscious, automatic doer. Just like a horse, once a movement is done, Self Two knows which muscles to use in order to do it again.

The problem is, Self One doesn't really trust Self Two to do the job properly, even though Self Two is extremely competent. So Self One starts trying very hard and thinking a lot, thus producing a lot of tension and muscle conflict. Then, of course, a mistake is made. Self One says, "See, I knew you couldn't do it on your own, stupid! Now, let's try harder this time." Our challenge, therefore, is to stop Self One from interfering with Self Two.

The main job of Self One is to set goals, that is, to communicate to Self Two what it wants and then to let Self Two do it. Just as the main job of a rider is to indicate to the horse what she wants from him and then to let the horse do it. Visualize it, feel it, repeat it a few times—then just let it happen.

The benefits to your riding come not from analyzing and instructing but from letting yourself absorb the mental images, then just doing it without conscious effort or control. Of course it would be silly to try to learn canter pirouettes this way; but if you break down the movement into small steps, then learning each one of those steps happens without much effort.

Gallwey also says every sporting activity is composed of two parts: an outer and an inner game. When applied to riding, the outer competition is to overcome external obstacles and to reach an external goal. The inner contest is the one that takes place in the mind of the rider and the struggle is against such obstacles as lapses in concentration, nervousness, self-doubt and self-condemnation. In short, we have to overcome all habits of mind that inhibit excellence in performance.

The smart rider comes to value relaxed concentration and learns that the true secret of winning lies not in trying hard but in being flexible.

Skills of the Smart Inner Rider

Not Blaming

Moralizing begins when something is labeled "bad" and causes interference with your riding. This leads to a need to find someone or something to blame. This causes a reaction of anger, frustration or disappointment.

Letting go of blame doesn't mean ignoring errors. It simply means seeing events as they are and not adding anything to them, then proceeding to modify them without emotional input. Moralistic labels such as good, bad, right or wrong, usually lead to emotional reactions, then to tightness, trying too hard, etc.

When we plant a seed in the earth we notice that it is small, but we don't criticize it as being "rootless and stemless." We treat it as a seed, giving it the water and nourishment required for it to grow. When it first shoots up out of the earth, we don't condemn it as immature and underdeveloped, nor do we criticize the buds for not being open when they appear. Similarly the errors we make can be seen as an important part of the developing process. They are not "bad" events.

Judgments are our personal, ego reactions to the sights, sounds, feelings and thoughts within our experiences. If you tell yourself often enough that you can't jump a two-foot, six-inch fence, a kind of hypnotic process takes place, and you become what you think. If, when you start working your horse, he doesn't respond precisely as you expected, you then judge him, form a moral opinion and become highly critical and tense. The next time the horse doesn't respond as expected, that proves your judgment was correct and the horse is, therefore, in a bad mood or not working well today. Many riders will not try an unfamiliar or new movement because they are afraid they probably will do it wrong and so damage the horse. While this is a commendable attitude, it is probably not founded in reality in most cases. Horses are very adaptable and very forgiving of our mistakes. The worst thing we can do is to rigidly repeat our mistakes or try to force the horse. If we want to try something new, it can be quite beneficial to experiment without force and without rigid repetition. While ideal conditions are very nice, the good horse-and-rider combination will be able to go in and out of occasional phases of imbalance, uncoordination and nonunderstanding, resulting in a better and more secure relationship. Incompetence does not mean lack of the essential action but consists largely in performing unnecessary movements.

Competence comes with the elimination of unnecessary movements

When the mind is free of any thought or blame, it is still and acts as a perfect mirror. Then and only then can we know things as they are. The moralistic mind distorts the perception of what actually happens. Trying to live up to expectations, standards of right and wrong interfere with learning and performing. Self One (and the left brain) always looks for approval and wants to avoid disapproval. When we are allowed to operate without interference from the conscious strivings of the subjective ego-mind, we perform much better.

Blame and negative evaluation are the enemies of self-motivation. They weaken our desire to improve. Instead, we wallow in self-pity over our inadequacy, fearing fresh challenges because they are likely to further reveal our incompetencies.

Many riders also judge themselves in anticipation of their instructor judging them to try and soften the blow. This is more a commentary on instruction methods than on the riders themselves.

There are usually many right ways to do most things. Perhaps more than any other sport, riding has a huge expectation of failure. This is because there are many ways to fail and the ways to succeed are not always apparent. The problem arises because of this multiplicity of choices, every horseperson being convinced that their way is the only right way. This leads to inflexibility and limiting beliefs associated with extremely fragile egos.

Riding is not a virtue; it isn't something that is morally good or bad. It is merely a skill that is in the process of being developed. The rider that has not developed sufficiently isn't unworthy, he is only at a stage of learning—just like everyone else.

A movement can be executed poorly or it can be executed well. Neither of these reflects on the worth of the rider; it just indicates how much more learning is needed. The rider with more learning isn't the superior being, she only knows a bit more about some things than some other riders.

If the rider attempts something new but doesn't quite succeed, the smart rider will not worry about it at all— they will acknowledge it, mentally improve it and do it again.

The key is to observe and modify, not judge.

Flexible Approach

If you are not getting the response you want, change your behavior.

To progress as a rider you need three things:

♦ Know what you want. Have a clear idea of what you'd like the outcome to be in any situation.

♦ Notice what you are getting. Be aware of the responses from the horse.

♦ Keep changing what you do until you get what you want.

Your ability to change your approach will guarantee success. Choosing to be flexible is choosing to achieve. If you have only one choice of action you are a robot. If you have two choices you have a dilemma. If you have more than two, you have flexibility.

Being flexible means being responsive to change and being adaptable. If what you are doing isn't getting the response you want, you can do something else that will. You can change your behavior until you get the response you want.

For example, if you ask your horse to move away from your leg and he doesn't, the correct response is not to kick harder. Better responses might be to change the way you ask (instead of the intensity), the timing of your aid, or the placement of your leg.

**If you always do what you always did,
you'll always get what you always got!**

Considering several different ways to respond besides your first reaction gives you power. For example, if your horse refuses a jump, your first response might be to punish your horse. If, instead, you choose another response, such as checking his feet, recalling if you might have been the cause, or looking to see if the ground underfoot was suitable, then you will have greater power. You will have the ability to progress beautifully with your horse, never acting violently or without thinking. The potential for more powerful responses lies in increased choices.

Stay Loose
Don't try harder, try softer.

Trying hard is one of the biggest errors we can make. When we try hard, we use more muscles than we need to, and we get tense. When we get tense nothing will work right.

Much of the difficulty in competitive riding lies not so much in the precision required, but in the task of releasing the tension that results from thinking how hard it is. Indicate and allow, instead of trying to make it happen.

Excess physical tension or stiffness is the contraction of too many muscles—more than are necessary to accomplish the task at hand. Then the tightness of some muscles will restrict the free movement of others. Attempting to remedy the problem by analyzing each instance of tightness is time-consuming and self-defeating. The best we can do is to be clear about our goal and to keep from interfering with its execution.

One good way to decrease tension is to increase it to the maximum extent and then let it go. Total body relaxation can be done on each part of the body in turn. For example, start with your hands. Make as tight a fist as you can, then let your hands relax. Continue this exercise on every body part. For a quick fix while riding, just lift the shoulders toward your ears and then let them drop.

When riders have their minds filled with too many commands, self-judgments, thoughts of doubt and fear of failure, they tend to ride poorly. The human brain can only focus on one thing at a time.

Head up ... heels down ... hands still ... inside leg on the girth ... outside leg behind the girth ... relax ...

Too many things to think about—this is not fun!

Yet when riding is a pleasure and gives a high of energy, their minds are relaxed, absorbed and quiet, free from these tensions. Often they say they weren't thinking at all.

Enjoy more, think less and ride better!

Naturally, it isn't possible to become a good rider by just having a good time and not thinking—we must always think, analyze, question and read. But when we are on the horse, we need to be aware of habitual mental patterns that are not constructive. Instead of trying to absorb many different things at the same time (which isn't possible), concentrate on just one at a time. Do this two or three times using your left brain, then switch sides and let the right brain take over—set it up, let it happen.

It has been said that when we are confronted with the unknown, we become tense. As our horse's reactions will often be unknown, especially when we are riding a green or unfamiliar horse, our natural instinct will be to become tense in order to protect ourselves. When you have an effective seat, you are able to control the horse with it, which, in turn, lets you stay untense and encourages the horse to relax and have confidence in you.

Don't Try Hard

The effects of self-doubt can be minimized if we try to see what is involved. Self-doubt tends to strengthen as the challenge increases and the most instinctual way of overcoming this strengthening doubt is to "try harder."

Since our culture praises achievement and censures laziness, most of us are encouraged by our parents, teachers and employers to control ourselves and exercise lots of willpower to overcome our shortcomings. When in doubt, try harder, they say. However, trying harder creates mental tension and conflict, which are reflected on a physical level as tightness or stiffness.

But how can we be better if we don't try harder? The most important action we can take is to try softer. The horse is a sensitive, subtle animal and often our heavy-handed behavior is incomprehensible to him. When we lighten up, our communication actually becomes much clearer to him, his tension goes away, and he can think again, thus giving the rider what she wants.

The second thing we can do is to visualize what we are trying to achieve, remembering that it is not the horse who is responsible for fixing problems; it is the rider. If you can visualize effectively, your body will respond well. One way to do this is to sit on the horse and visualize the movement as it should be and then start again. Or you can do something else totally different and then come back to the problem when you are calmer. Or you could do something easy, finish the lesson, visualize that night and come back to the problem at the next session.

Set It Up and Let It Happen

When we have trust in ourselves and our horses, we can stay flexible and loose. Tell your right brain what you want, and let it happen. Indicate to the horse what you want, and then let it happen.

The key word here is "let"—let yourself sit in the saddle. Let your legs hang down naturally. Let the horse see the jump and do it. Letting it happen is not *making it happen* and it is not *trying hard*. If your body knows how to ride a corner, then just let it happen; if it doesn't, then help it learn and then let it happen.

As we practice, the right brain refines and extends the information in its memory bank. So the important thing to remember whenever learning something is to allow the natural learning process to take place and to forget about many self-instructions.

Find out the difference between *making* something happen and *allowing* it to happen. Experience the happiness of *allowing* the horse to learn, as compared to *making* it learn.

Knowing the secrets of being able to control your emotions will give you strength and power. But that isn't enough—we also have to be able to manage ...

Chapter 5
TIME:
A SCARCE RESOURCE

We have enough time if we but use it right.
—Unknown

If you say to yourself, "I want to ride, but I just don't have the time," perhaps you might take a closer look at how you spend your time.

Dennis Piggott was an Australian Olympic representative in eventing. Before he was recognized as an elite rider, he helped his father run a newsagency in Sydney. Naturally, this meant getting up very early in the morning. So, in order to keep improving his riding he got up even earlier and made sure he rode before he went to work. That was many years ago before "time management" became a skill that could be studied and developed. Despite this, Dennis was obviously dedicated enough to manage his time effectively so his riding wouldn't suffer because of his other commitments.

Learn how to make the most of every hour—eliminate time-wasting activities so you have time for your real priorities.

Analyze

If you kept a time log of your day and saw how you used your time, you would probably get a shock as to how much time has just slipped through your fingers!

Try keeping track of your day. If you are the kind of person who writes things down, divide your page into 15-minute intervals. At the end of each hour, record how that hour was spent. Use codes like: TV (television), HW (housework), K (kids), G (garden), Th (thinking), T (telephone), Re (reading), TR (travelling), Ri (riding). This will probably take fewer than five minutes a day and will be very revealing.

Some people will not want to actually write these things down. If you are one of those people who can recall accurately what has happened during the day and for approximately how long, do the same exercise in your head.

How long is your 15-minute coffee break? How long were you listening to chatter on the phone? How long did it take to do the shopping? You may find that you have no idea of how your time is really spent. Memory isn't entirely to be trusted in this area as we tend to recall the productive hours of the day and to push time wasted into the background. "Doing nothing" isn't necessarily time wasted—often it is time being used to rest, or to think, both of which are productive.

After keeping a log for three or four days, you may begin to notice opportunities for improvement. After a week you will probably see that the tasks you consider to be the most important are consuming the least number of hours.

Organize

Remember Murphy's Law:

♦ Nothing is as simple as it seems.
♦ Everything takes longer than it should.
♦ If anything can go wrong, it will.

When you are planning ahead, organizing your time, always allow for Murphy's Law. Don't necessarily plan down to the last minute because when something unexpected happens, this will throw your whole schedule out, create stress, upset other people and convince you that planning ahead doesn't work.

But planning does work—as long as you allow for the unexpected. If it takes you an hour to get your horse on the trailer and to the venue, allow an hour and a half (because Murphy's Law will rule). If you know you can saddle up and work your horse in 45 minutes, allow an hour. If you always allow extra time when you are organizing your day, life will be less stressful and you will feel more in control.

Planning is a big part of organization especially when it involves horses. In order to achieve peak performance and efficiency, we have to do a lot of thinking, and most of this thinking should be done ahead of time. We should think about our goals and how to achieve them; we should also think a lot about what we are going to do when we ride.

Planning and preparation are very important—they help to organize our lives, giving us our direction and helping us to achieve our goals. We have to plan what time we will ride and then we have to plan the way in which we will school the horse (warming up, revising the previous session, working on new stuff, cooling down); we have to plan the week—which days will have hard work, which day will be a relaxing day (a trail ride) and which will be our lesson day.

Once we have decided what we are going to work on, we then have to think how we are going to do it—how to break it down into small chunks; how to avoid mistakes; how to avoid resistances.

Prioritize

The president of a big investment firm in the United States called in a consultant and asked him to show him a way to get more things done with his time. In return, he said he would pay the consultant any fee within reason. The consultant gave him a blank piece of paper and told the president to write down the six most important tasks he had to do the next day and number them in order of importance. Then, first thing in the morning look at item one and start working on it until it was finished. Then do item two and so on. Do this until quitting time, and don't be concerned if you have only finished items 1 or 2. Then on tomorrow's list put the uncompleted items at the top of the list and add your next most important tasks until you have six tasks on your list for each day. Do this every working day. If a task is on your list for more than a week, forget it.

Several weeks later the president sent the consultant a check for $25,000, saying it was the most profitable advice he had ever had.

Important or Urgent?

Distinguish between actions that are *important* and those that are *urgent*. A priority may have different mixes of these two ingredients—usually the important things are more critical than the urgent ones. Quite often it is easy to get trapped by a multitude of urgent tasks and that's when we can feel overwhelmed as if we'll never be able to get everything done. In these situations, often the best thing to do is nothing. It's amazing how often things will sort themselves out if we just leave them alone.

The important tasks do have to be done, but if you have prioritized and organized properly, you will be able to handle these. Tasks which are both urgent and important must be attended to at once.

You have to decide which goals are most crucial to your overall happiness. And remember that a top priority also can be to have some quality time of your own. These things don't always have to be serious or virtuous.

Setting priorities is simply a matter of putting first things first. You can number them in order of importance, or group them in the "A-B-C method:"

A—Must do: things that are important and urgent
B—Should do: things that are important
C—Nice to do: other things that can be done at any time

Of course, if you are ambitious, riding will always be **A—Must do**.

Another way to set priorities is to color code the list— underline or highlight the top-priority items in one color; use another color for the medium-priority, etc.

Learn to Say No

Overcommitment is one of the most frequent ways we dilute our effectiveness. Devoting a little of ourself to many things means we aren't able to commit a great deal of ourself to anything. We are left unable to concentrate on the important goals.

We usually say yes, even when we know it is our best interests to say no. For two reasons: (1) We are afraid someone will have a lesser opinion of us, or (2) Answering a request for our help indulges our ego by giving us a feeling of power.

When we say yes because we have need for approval, we are in effect saying to ourselves that someone else's opinion of us is more important than our own opinion. You can learn to live without depending on others for approval. It's nice when it happens, but it's weak to base your decisions on what others want.

- Make a point to politely and directly refuse requests that are not in your best interest. Learning to say no is like learning to swim—you increase your proficiency with practice.

- Say it at once—don't raise people's hopes by saying, "I don't know" or "I'll think about it."

- Realize that you have the right to say no without needing to give a reason.

- Be polite and pleasant.

Value Quality Time

Quality time is time we spend that is productive or rewarding. If it is time you want to spend with your children, it is special, so don't allow it to be frittered away. When it is time for them, it is time for them and not gossiping on the phone, having a bath or gardening. That time is valuable and is not to be intruded upon by less valuable things.

It is just the same with riding—if you have organized your day so that you can ride for an hour at 3:00, then when 3:00 comes, make sure you are riding, not talking, shopping, oiling your saddle, or anything else.

We need to be aware of our own time-wasting activities. Of course, sometimes we all procrastinate with our riding because of one thing or another. Maybe we are experiencing a temporary lack of confidence; maybe we are feeling time-pressured in our other activities; or perhaps we are going to have to confront a situation when we actually start working the horse.

If your time to ride is approaching and you have some unfinished tasks, put them aside until after you have ridden. If you are in the middle of a conversation, end it, because you have something important to do. If you are tired, remind yourself that riding will energize you; if you are stressed, remember that riding is the best therapy.

If you are in two minds as to whether to ride or not, let this help you to decide:

◆ If you ride, your horse will immediately **develop** more strength and muscle.

◆ If you don't ride, your horse will immediately **lose** strength and muscle.

Smart riding is always productive and therefore must always be rewarding—don't deny yourself the opportunity to feel good and also to achieve something for you and your horse. At this point you're ready to move on to the next section of this book. You've learned the fundamental tools for shaping your life and taking control of it.

Now let's look at the specific tools needed to become a good rider. The first and most important step is to understand as much as possible about your horse....

Chapter 6

UNDERSTANDING YOUR HORSE

All horses are infinitely improvable.
—Charles de Kunffy

Horse Psychology

Temperament

Horses are programmed and built to run—their best defense from predators.They aren't good at fighting, although they will if they have to. Given a choice, they would sooner avoid confrontation. So their temperament basically inclines them to extreme caution, sensitivity, acute awareness of surroundings and any changes. Horses that are in a safe environment are also curious, placid, trainable and friendly. Very few horses are born mean, aggressive or nasty—mostly they are made that way by people.

Horses generally can be divided into three classes according to temperament:

♦ **hot blooded** (Arabians and Thoroughbreds)—very sensitive, fine skin and coat, intelligent, fast reactions, can be nervous. Usually if breeders want to improve their stock, they will add some hot blood.

♦ **cold blooded** (draft and heavy horses)—steady, easy to get along with, coarse skin and coat, strong.

♦ **warm blooded**—neither a hot blood nor a cold blood. The term originates from the German *Warmblut*, meaning manageable temperament. The warmblood has

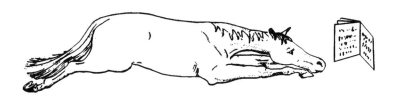

Hitting the books!

always been defined by geographical area, with foals being registered where they are born. The distinguishing feature of warmbloods is that they are specifically bred by selective methods to produce an athletic, sound horse with a good temperament. (Definition adapted from *The International Warmblood Horse*, by D. Wallin, J. Kidd and C. Clarke, Kenilworth Press, 1995).

Intelligence

Horses learn very quickly and have extremely good memories—two characteristics of intelligence. However, horses aren't good at logical reasoning and this is where horses differ from human beings and possibly some other primates. Horses have different instincts, needs and motivations from humans, therefore their mental processes are different. If a horse wants to get from point A to point B, he will try and take the most direct straight line, even if that is through a fence, whereas a human will work out the most effective way.

A lot of the behavior of the horse is attributable to causes that we as humans aren't even aware of. They can hear things we can't, they see things in a different way from us and they are programmed to run away from frightening or unknown things. Because we aren't aware of these things, we often interpret their behavior wrongly.

Trainability

In 400 B.C. Xenophon said, *"A horse should be trained so that he looks forward to his time spent with man."* Horses have a herd instinct—they prefer to be part of a group and that group will have a very defined pecking order, from the boss (most dominant) right down to the youngest/weakest/smallest/most timid.

As trainers we are able to take advantage of these instincts. It isn't difficult to establish yourself as herd leader—the fact that you are able to put on a halter or bridle and control the movement of the horse makes you a leader. If you can walk beside him and then stop him by turning your body toward his, you are the boss. Subtle things like this mean a lot to a horse and if we realize the power they give us on the ground, we don't have to try so hard when we are mounted.

Quick Learners

Horses learn very quickly—in fact they are learning all the time. Sometimes we teach them things without knowing and often these things can be things we would rather the horse hadn't learned, because later on we will have to remedy that situation. For example, you may be working with a young horse and you walk up to him in the paddock to put on the halter and lead rope. The horse moves away, realizes he can and moves farther. He has learned that if he doesn't want to be caught he can elude you. This is not a good thing for the horse to learn. Better to have him confined in a pen, then teach him that if you want to catch him, you will and there is nowhere for him to go.

The memory of the horse seems to be closely associated with emotions. Things that frighten him or things that make him feel good are what he will remember. We want to avoid frightening the horse because he will never forget that fear or what caused it. Instead we should be instilling habits and good memories which are based on reactions that are rewarded.

Latent Learners

Horses seem to consolidate learning when they are left alone for a while—this is latent learning. For example, if you have been practicing a new movement and stop as soon as the horse shows some understanding, then the next time you ride, the horse seems to have absorbed the lesson and does the movement even better than before.

Because horses are quick and latent learners, it makes sense to be very aware of the horse's understanding of the lesson and not to belabor the point by mindless repetition or by repeating it until it is perfect. The quality of the lesson learned is much more likely to be excellent if you get off on a good note and return to the same exercise one or two days later.

"Little and often" is the phrase we must bear in mind all the time when training the horse.

Relaxed Learners

One of the most important things to remember when training a horse is that if he is not relaxed he won't learn anything. If his body is tense, his brain will be blocked as well and nothing will get in. You waste your time and energy by trying and will probably escalate the situation by getting forceful because of your frustration.

In order for the horse to learn, you must have his attention. This is something that the horse can only give to you, not something you can *make* him do or that you can *take* from him. And if you want him to give you his attention, you have to be a bit clever and divert or redirect his focus by coaxing and encouragement, gradually. Don't expect that because the horse is amenable most of the time, he will be instantly concentrated on you whenever you choose—you may have to put some time into preparation, or do some work that requires concentration, like changing direction, transitions and lateral work combined with lengthening work. Sometimes a good canter can clear out the cobwebs, then the horse will settle down.

Why is My Horse Calm Until I Get On Him?

Tests and research have shown that the pulse rate of a horse doubles when the rider mounts him. The adrenaline rate increases and this has the effect of making the horse a bit spooky at first. The way to counteract this is to be patient and not asking anything of him in the first five minutes. Let him get into the attentive frame of mind that you want; don't try and force it or it will take 15 minutes instead of five.

If your horse is very nervous about, for example crossing water for the first time, get off and his heart rate will go down. Then when he is calm, lead him across the creek. The lesson learned will then be that the water is not, after all, something to be afraid of. The next time should be easier and the time after that will probably not be a problem at all.

Understanding this enables us to teach the horse many things without having to resort to force.

How Do We Teach the Horse to Focus?

If you are going to teach the horse something, you must have his attention or he won't learn. Therefore, getting the attention of the horse, or training him to focus, must be one of your aims when warming up.

109

Start with a structured, consistent warm-up routine; one which is done every time you ride. Use exercises which you have thought about in advance and planned. For example, start with walking and trotting on a loose rein for a few minutes, then gradually take up the contact and do some bending work, such as figure eights or small serpentines.

When his head is slightly to the inside with the nose below the horizontal and you have his ears coming back to you and his eyes steady, you are on the way. Will he lower his head and neck to the ground and still keep contact? Are you getting an immediate response to your leg aids? If so, he is starting to concentrate. When he audibly breathes out, he is relaxing—this is also an aid to focusing.

How Do Horses Learn?

Reward

To the horse, a reward can be one of many different things. One of the most obvious is stroking or a scratch, another is by voice—a soothing or encouraging tone; the cessation of pressure is another form of reward, for example, when we stop pulling on the reins.

It is important to remember when rewarding the horse that

- ✦ the reward must be immediate (within one second of the action), or the horse will not associate the reward with the action, and
- ✦ the reward must be consistent—always the same gesture, tone of voice, or words.

Another form of reward is to *get off*—this is why we always try to finish a session on a good note and reward that by dismounting. And, like us, horses will remember well the last thing they learned.

Repetition

Some repetition is necessary for horses to learn, but not nearly as much as most people think. When the horse has done something right, doing that thing right twice more and then stopping is usually sufficient. Often we repeat things ad nauseam, more for our own benefit than the horse's. After a while, the horse will switch off and go around on automatic, not learning or remembering anything.

Observation

Horses learn very quickly by observing other horses or even people they respect. For example, when teaching a horse to trot on the leadline, we actually go from a walk to a run (trot) ourselves and the horse then trots after observing us. Often a young horse will watch an older one being trained and learn quite a lot of what the older one was doing.

Physical Pressure

Horses move away from intermittent pressure. If we press on his side, he will move his side away from that pressure. If we apply pressure with the rein on the neck, he will move his neck away.

If we use pressure on the girth with our inside leg, the horse has no alternative but to move his girth away from that pressure. If we apply pressure with both legs, the horse should go forward in order to move away from that pressure.

Pulling on the reins creates pain in the horse's mouth—a pressure he would like to move away from. So it is obvious that this is not the best way to get a horse to stop. He stops because he has learned that when he stops, the pain stops. We could just as easily teach him to stop by tweaking his ear or pinching his wither.

If the pressure is consistent and lasts for a while, the horse will be inclined to lean into it, instead of moving away from it. This is especially obvious if you apply pressure to the side of the horse—he will lean toward the pressure in order to avoid falling over. If the rider applies continuous pressure through the bit onto the bars of the mouth, the horse will either lean on the bit or withdraw from any contact with it. Both are protective devices from pain.

The young or green horse needs to do a lot of long and low work

The horse is built to go forward. Even when in dressage they appear to be going sideways such as in half pass, they must still be going forward as well. To move only sideways is contrary to the way the horse is built and sooner or later will be counter-productive. Lateral movements must be regular and rhythmical, and are designed to improve collection, balance and paces. If the the horse doesn't go forward as well as sideways, these outcomes can't be achieved.

The Thighbone's Connected to the Hipbone

Muscles consist of parallel bunches of long fibers and long tendons. Some muscles can lengthen and shorten to a very considerable extent and are responsible for movement. They are designed so that they can contract and relax rapidly.

If these muscles have to maintain tension, waste products rapidly accumulate among the fibers, resulting in stiffness and pain. Conversely, alternating between relaxation and contraction promotes good circulation and rapid excretion of waste products.

On the other hand, *postural* muscles (consisting of short fibers) contract and relax slowly and can maintain tension with less expenditure of energy.

Every muscle has an opposing partner that restores it to its resting length following contraction. Sometimes muscles whose primary function is to flex or extend joints, must also behave like elastic suspenders and shock absorbers.

Although exercise develops the strength and bulk of muscles, this only happens provided that they function in the manner for which their structure is fitting. If muscles which are designed for movement have to maintain continuous tension, they become inflamed. This creates pain, which often results in behavioral issues.

The Importance of the Back Muscles

Back muscles have two main functions:
1. to make the vertebral column sufficiently rigid.
2. to transmit energy from the hindquarters to the front legs.

Contraction of any individual group of muscles in the back extends to all the associated groups. If the rider inflicts discomfort to one part, the activity of all the muscles of the back is affected and as these are connected to the neck, head, back and front legs, the smoothness and the efficiency of movement is impaired.

Untrained or badly trained horses never learn to use their backs elastically and stiffen as soon as they are asked to work, making their gait unsteady and irregular. This makes it impossible for the rider to sit easily to the trot or to keep his balance without gripping. This is why rising trot is important when starting to train or retrain a horse. For the same reason, a rider who relies on gripping to safeguard balance will never be able to feel, preserve and promote the essential elasticity of the back muscles of the horse.

The Head and Neck Muscles

The horse's muscles that brace the vertebral column so it can support the weight of the rider are in the neck. The *nuchal ligament* (which is like an elastic band going from the skull to the withers, then along the spine to the tailbone) is also involved. Therefore the rider should sit as close as possible to the pommel of the saddle, to facilitate the task of the neck muscles.

At the beginning of training, it is gravity working on the weight of the head that tenses the neck muscles. The distance between the poll and the withers must be as great as possible. Eventually the neck muscles will gain strength and their elastic tension will then allow a relative elevation of the neck. As the hind muscles develop and can take more weight, the forehand becomes lighter and the neck will become more able to raise itself. This is a natural consequence of correct work and can't be done properly any other way. Since the neck muscles are inserted at the poll, the horse's nose will drop vertically.

The incorrect short neck with the nose behind the vertical

The correct long neck with the nose in front of the
vertical.

If the rider actively holds up the neck, the neck muscles
must shorten and the back and neck muscles will become
weaker. The horse will probably put his head behind the
vertical and will try and avoid the strong contact with the
rider's hands. So when the horse is allowed to lower his
neck, the muscles of the back can then, instead of sup-

porting the rider, perform the task for which they were designed: the transmission of energy from the hind limbs to the forelimbs.

The Shape of the Neck

The shape of the neck of the trained horse reveals more about the quality of the training than any other part of the body. When a horse works efficiently, the muscles of the topline of the neck are supporting a heavy load and grow in bulk and strength. Since the muscles underneath the neck remain inactive, they atrophy. So the top of the neck is curved and the underneath part follows a similar line (concave, not convex).

An over-developed underneck muscle is proof of incorrect training

The outline of the vertebral column itself also changes as the muscles of the neck become stronger and pull up the last cervical and first thoracic vertebrae, with the consequence of the neck becoming regularly arched, with the hollow in front of the withers gradually disappearing as training progresses. The whole neck will become longer. It is the lengthening contraction of the powerful neck muscles resisting the pull of gravity that eventually ensures the firm connection of the base of the neck with the withers.

Whenever the horse's nose is behind the vertical, he is not only restricted from moving forward but he can't see where he is going if his nose is on or behind the vertical. Alison Harman, from the University of Western Australia, has been researching the eye of the horse and has discovered that the horse can only see in the direction his nose is pointing.

When riders fix their hands to enforce a vertical position of the nose, they not only prevent movement of the head and neck, but they also prevent engagement of the hind legs. These fixed hands also cause compression of the glands behind the horse's jaw, resulting in the his trying to avoid discomfort by poking out his nose (thus shortening the muscles of the topline of the neck), or by contracting the jaw muscles to hold his mouth open or to lock his jaws.

The mandibular (jaw) muscles and the muscles attached to the tongue are connected to the muscles of the neck, body and shoulders. If only one muscle in this group is contracted, the stiffness is communicated to the poll, neck and shoulders and then to the back and hind quarters.

Conversely, pain in the region of the back is reflected by the tightening of the muscles of the jaw and tongue as well as by restriction of the forward engagement of the hind legs. Relaxation of all those muscles, free forward movement, and the elastic tension of the muscles of the topline are completely related. The neck of the horse must be firmly stabilized by the firmness of the muscles which attach it to the withers. It is their tone which enables the head to remain steady.

Freedom of the Shoulder

For the horse to be straight, the neck must be straight. However, it is always wrong to enforce straightness by using constraining reins and hands. Freedom of shoulder movement is essential and this depends entirely on the absence of restraining influences of hands and reins. The horse must be allowed to move so it can develop the muscles necessary for more advanced work.

Neck carriage determines the movement of the front legs. When the neck muscles are lengthened, the forelimb can extend farther. If these muscles are shortened, the horse throws up his head and is difficult to control. A shortened neck impacted between the shoulders restricts the play of the shoulder joint and shortens the steps.

When jumping, a horse can land safely only if he can extend a foreleg well forward and this is possible only if he has complete freedom of the neck. When performing lateral movements, the dressage horse can only move forward and sideways properly if his neck is not contracted.

Loosening the Horse's Back

The horse's back and croup muscles must work in harmony because they share a common attachment. The hind legs cannot swing freely if the back muscles are insufficiently active and the back muscles can't work properly if the rider prevents the freedom of movement of the hind limbs.

Stiffness of the main back muscles affects the elasticity of the muscle that connects the back to the upper forelegs, and this consequently prevents the free forward swing of the front leg. Thus, freedom of the shoulder depends on the free activity of the back muscles.

As the back muscles are also connected to the ribs, the respiratory movements of the rib cage will be inhibited if the back muscles are stiff. A tense horse holds his breath, but audible blowing shows that he is loosening up.

One of the main causes of improper tension of the horse's back muscles is a rider with a rigidly straight back—one reflects the other. Sitting trot should not be used before the horse's back muscles are strong enough and have relaxed, inviting the rider to sit. When the rider then does sitting trot, his lower back should be supple enough to absorb the horse's movement.

The back muscles are also muscles for movement, and their elasticity must never be impaired by the effort of carrying the weight of a rider who clamps the saddle with the strength of his legs. Because of the relationship between the major back muscles to the hind limbs and forelimbs, the back is totally involved in the movements of all the limbs.

A jerky trot that tosses the rider is not necessarily an incurable peculiarity of the horse but is often a symptom of tightly contracted and insufficiently active back muscles. A springy, ground covering trot shows proper elastic tension of the back muscles.

Frequent periods of cantering and galloping are the best way of loosening stiff backs and strengthening weak ones, because in those gaits, contraction and relaxation of the muscles occur on both sides of the back and the lengthening and shortening of the muscles are greater.

Flexion of the Hindquarters

The hindquarters not only propel the horse's body forward but also act as shock absorbers by bending at the hip, stifle and hock at the moment when it has to support the weight. This phase of the movement is the one that puts the greatest stress on the muscles of the hindquarters. Obtaining flexion of the hindquarters without impairing impulsion is very difficult because it requires effort from the horse that he doesn't particularly want to make.

The muscles of the hindquarters are mainly for movement—they have very little tendinous reinforcement and are therefore not ideally designed for sustaining tension. For this reason, they must be carefully developed by progressive training.

Increased flexion of the hock delays propulsion, which means that much more muscular effort is required to drive the hind leg back. Eventually the rider wants to prolong this phase so he can impart more spring and energy into the movement.

The stifle and hock joints are tied together in such a manner that one joint can't flex or extend unless the other does the same.

Prolonged resistance of the hands always provokes the horse into stiffening the supporting legs, resulting either in running away or insufficient forward movement, trying to avoid the pressure. A horse constantly on guard can't swing his limbs in an easy rhythmical manner.

To avoid this stiffness the correct method is to use half halts, but only when the horse has done enough free forward training to be balanced and to respond correctly.

Muscular Training of the Horse

At the beginning of training it is *propelling* power that must be developed, and the gaits must be free, easy and rhythmical. One should not start the gymnastic flexing of the haunches or try to slow the speed by means of half halts on taut reins before the hindquarters are sufficiently strong and the horse is capable of walking, trotting and cantering in natural balance, that is, without seeking support of the reins and without overloading the forehand.

Applying a lower leg aid stimulates the muscles around the horse's ribs, which flex the hip joint and draw the hind limb forward. This is a reflex action, but if the aid is a constant hard squeeze, the horse will push against it or draw away from it. The rider, therefore, needs to use only light and intermittent leg aids; if the horse doesn't respond, then the whip should be immediately applied at the girth. There is no point in thumping the horse or jumping up and down in the saddle—these actions will have only detrimental effects.

There is a small area of skin just behind the girth that is so sensitive to the slightest pressure of the lower leg it is called the "neuralgic spot," but this will only be responsive as long as the rider hasn't deadened the area through bashing the sides of the horse.

Immediate Response

Some horses have very quick reactions and others are slow. If we are using horses to pull a plow, we need strength, not fast reactions. If we are teaching a disabled person to ride, we must have a horse with slow reactions. If we are doing dressage, we need to be riding a horse that will respond immediately to the lightest touch of our leg. The more immediate the response required, the more Arabian and/or Thoroughbred blood there needs to be in the horse. Therefore, for dressage, we should look for a horse with "blood." Of course, a pony or draft horse is capable of doing dressage up to a certain level, but when precision and instant reactions are needed, such as at the higher level tests, those types are often not suitable. The more dependable and docile horses have slower response times and are therefore better suited to strength and reliability needs.

Lameness

Lameness implies pain or mechanical dysfunction and is most readily assessed at the walk or the trot, rarely at the canter. It occurs more often in the fore limbs than the hindlimbs and more often below the knee than above it. Many horses are able to work satisfactorily despite low-grade lameness, especially in the hindlimb. Lameness, however subtle, is unacceptable in any performance horse.

Diagnosis

Diagnosing lameness begins by watching and listening to the horse on a hard level ground. Listen for irregular footfalls and watch for irregular limb flight, the length of stride, the degree of joint movement, and head carriage.

- The head will rise as the lame leg hits the ground and nod as the sound leg is on the ground.

- The horse will land more heavily on the sound leg.

- If the lameness involves the hindquarters, the lame leg will have a shorter stride than the sound one; the leg may move stiffly or drag the toe; there may be asymmetrical movement of the hindquarters, with the hip of the lame leg rising and falling more than the sound one.

- If the horse points a front foot this could indicate pain at the back of or underneath the foot.

Treatment

Many kinds of lameness respond to rest, but if it is pronounced, such as when the horse will not put any weight on it at all or lasts for a long while, a vet should be called in.

After injury there is generally pain, localized heat and swelling; treatment is aimed at reducing these. Cold treatment tends to reduce soft tissue swelling; heat tends to increase the blood supply to the area. Administering pain killers is usually not recommended, as this could aggravate the injury when the horse becomes more active due to the lack of pain.

Conformation

The ideal conformation for a horse will differ according to the kind of work it is required to do. Horses that pull heavy loads should have more upright shoulders, hocks close together, short pasterns and necks. None of these would be desirable conformation points for a pleasure or show horse.

Good conformation implies that the transmission of energy will not be impeded. If the front legs are knock kneed, energy will be wrongly used to compensate for the break in a straight line, instead of for forward movement. So in a performance horse, we should look for straight legs from the side, the front and the back.

Some horses manage to be very fast and do it on legs that go in four different directions—this is probably because of their own willpower or nervous energy. These horses are unlikely to be sound as they get older and may be prone to arthritis or other ailments.

It is reasonable to state that the closer the horse's conformation is to ideal, the more sound he will be, according to the type of work it does. Of course, if a horse is subjected to work that he is not fit for (because he is too

young, or out of condition, etc), he will probably break down.

How much variation is acceptable?

Any extreme deviation will result in unsoundness or poor movement. If the neck is very short, the shoulder very sloping, the pasterns very long or short, the back very long or short, any of these can cause problems. A short neck can't be lengthened. A weak back can't be improved.

When moving, if there is any deviation from straight (front legs dishing, paddling, hind legs traveling wide, etc) or symmetrical (uneven trot or walk), this could indicate potential problems in the future.

However, often a horse which has a conformation totally unsuitable to be competitive in a particular discipline might have a wonderful temperament and be could ideal for teaching beginners. Horses that do work that requires medium demands on them physically can often have many conformation faults and still perform extremely well. However, when horses are involved in work that demands extreme pressures on them physically, such as national or international competition, good conformation becomes very important.

Feeding and Nutrition

The principles of feeding for horses are very different from those of feeding other animals. Most animals, when given more food than they require for normal needs, will use that extra food to produce milk, meat, fat, or wool. Horses, however, were never designed by nature to use excess feed in the production of anything but energy and heat. If we overfeed horses in relation to their actual requirements, we will end up with either a sick horse or one that is difficult to control.

Horses need energy in the form of carbohydrates, protein and fats, as well as vitamins and minerals. Generally, mature horses can maintain themselves and perform moderate exercise for short periods on good quality pasture alone. When pasture is sparse or of poor nutritional quality, hay can be used as a supplement. Performance horses need extra nutrients.

Energy

Nature has designed the horse to use energy for action and heat. Therefore any energy fed in excess of that needed for heat, growth and maintenance has to be used by the horse as a fuel for exercise and activity.

Protein

Protein is found in all feeds, but the highest concentrations are in grains and seeds. Proteins are required for growth (hooves, hair, muscles, blood, skin) and repair (injuries). A percentage of 10 to 12 is good—there is no advantage to feeding higher percentages. It has been shown that feeding excessive protein can increase heart and respiratory rates and the horse will also urinate more, necessitating a greater water intake.

When the horse is doing more exercise, you don't need to feed more protein, you need to feed more feed—the horse will then automatically get the additional protein in the correct ratios. Good quality grain or related feeds and good alfalfa hay will have the right amount of proteins.

Carbohydrates

Carbohydrates are the main source of energy and come mainly from cereal grains, and can only be absorbed from the small intestine. The breakdown of fiber occurs in the large intestine and produces heat. The less fiber there is, the less heating occurs.

Fats

Fats come mainly from grains and seeds, but vegetable oils are also sometimes used. Oils are good but expensive and can go rancid quickly.. Fats release energy more slowly than carbohydrates and proteins in aerobic activity, so they do not cause as much hyperactivity as grains.

Use of Energy

Any horse that is trained well, with his muscles conditioned to use energy in the presence of oxygen, can work aerobically for longer periods before he reaches the anaerobic threshold. In other words, correct training procedures need to be integrated with correct feeding techniques to get the best results.

Lactic acid is the end product resulting from the use of energy in the muscles. The level of lactic acid increases considerably when the horse goes at medium canter or faster, but if the horse has been trained and conditioned correctly he will have 50 percent less lactic acid accumulation during and after exercise.

After working it is important for the horse to cool down for about 10 minutes so as to get rid of the lactic acid. If not, the horse could get stiff or tie up.

Excess Energy

Excess carbohydrate energy can be retained in the horse as glycogen, being stored in the muscles or the liver, or else converted into fat as part of the horse's internal fat deposits. Once stored inside the horse, energy can only be used for muscle activity.

When the horse increases muscle size, his body lays down fat inside the muscle, but rarely on the outside of the muscles. When one "fattens" up a horse, this generally means building up the muscles. If the amount of energy stored as fat reaches a saturation point, the horse is unable to convert any more carbohydrate energy to fat or to store any more energy as fat. Then the additional energy has to be released from the horse, either as a disorder such as founder, tying up, or colic, etc., or as behavioral problems.

Vitamins

If the mineral intake is correct, additional vitamins will rarely be necessary. Behind every vitamin deficiency there is usually a mineral one. A deficiency disease can develop if the intake of essential vitamins is inadequate or reduced.

If a horse is given phenylbutazone (bute) or antibiotics, he should also get additional Vitamin C, because bute could cause internal bleeding and antibiotics upset the internal balance.

Minerals

The mineral content of the soil determines the amount of minerals in feed. Minerals and trace elements are essential for skeletal development and maintenance. Soil deficiencies and natural imbalances reduce the certainty that horses will get sufficient levels. On the other hand, excess supplementation often can be toxic and/or interfere with the absorption of other minerals or vitamins.

Seaweed meal has all minerals and trace elements in organic form and in balance. It is also a natural source of biotin, which strengthens the hooves. The average dose for a 1,000-pound horse is about a teaspoon per day. There is no exact dose, but too much can be harmful.

Calcium/Phosphorus Ratio

The calcium/phosphorus ratio of your horse's diet should be about 2:1. Adequate bone growth is a function of the correct amounts of calcium, phosphorus and Vitamin D (sunlight). Deficiency of any of these may result in lameness, reduced performance, sway back, crooked legs and often in conditions that have no obvious symptoms until too late.

A good quality alfalfa hay contains correct amounts of calcium and phosphorus. However, there are some conditions that inhibit the absorption of calcium, making it necessary to give a supplement. Dolomite is the best calcium supplement—give about a tablespoon per day for a 1,000-pound horse, less for smaller ones and ponies. Dolomite also contains magnesium, which is necessary for the absorption of calcium and also for bone growth, muscular health and the nervous system. Many pasture areas and therefore feeds are deficient in magnesium.

Grains are high in phosphorus, so if grain constitutes significantly more than half the feed, give dolomite as a supplement.

Recognizing Signs of Physical Condition

♦ A horse in poor condition has his spine, ribs and other bones protruding.

♦ A horse in good condition has the spine covered, with his spine not protruding and his ribs are not seen.

♦ A fat horse has an obvious crease down his back, lumps of fat over the body and his buttocks rubbing together.

Recognizing Signs of Work

These signs relate generally to a horse that is not fit:

♦ When the horse has done light work, there may be some sweating around the neck and a slight increase in the breathing rate.

128

♦ Medium work produces sweating on the neck, chest and flanks. Some veins are showing, breath ing is increased. Recovery takes about five min- utes.

♦ Hard work produces sweat on the neck and body. Veins are protruding. Breathing is heavy. Recovery rate is about 10 minutes.

Sweating patterns can also indicate where the horse is using his muscles the most: when sweating is seen around the neck and shoulders, this indicates that the horse has been using his forehand muscles a lot. This would occur on a green horse or one that isn't being trained properly. (Neck sweating can also indicate a nervous energy being used). The fitter the horse is, the less it will sweat.

A General Feeding Guide

As a rule of thumb, a 1,000 pound horse (average 16h) at rest needs about 20 to 25 pounds of feed per day, as half green (hay) and half grain (by weight). As the work increases to medium intensity, the grain should increase to about two-thirds the whole ration.

♦ If the work is increased, feed more.

♦ If the feed is increased, work more.

A pony of half the weight needs half the ration and probably no grain. A larger pony or small horse needs about three-quarters of the ration, depending on the work.

With horses, nothing should be done suddenly.

The bacteria and enzymes in the horse's digestive tract are specific to the type of feed the horse is used to. Horses can't adjust overnight; it usually takes a period of days and sometimes weeks.

♦ If the feed is to be changed drastically, do it gradually over one to weeks.

♦ If you are going to increase the horse's work, take four to five weeks to toughen his legs and increase his fitness before doing medium-intensity work.

♦ When the work is decreased, let the horse down gradually over three to four weeks, feeding less grain until maintenance rations are reached.

Hay
Good hay is green inside, stems about four to five inches long and not too rigid. The leaf sticks to the stems and some flower can be seen.

Poor hay is brittle and brownish, with the leaf falling off the stem. It has long hard stems, no flowers and often contains foreign matter such as thistles, burrs, etc.

Grain
Oats are the most efficient—lots of fiber and lowest energy. They should smell clean, look a good oaten color and be plump with no dust.

Barley has more energy and is lower in fiber than oats, but has a tougher seed coat. This means that barley has to be boiled or cracked, or most of it will pass through the horse. If it is boiled, some nutrients are lost. If cracked, it should be done on the day of feeding, or the grain will oxidize and again lose nutrients. Bran has high sulfur content, and its calcium/phosphorus ratio is 1:11 (bad).

At this point you're ready to move on to the next section of this book. You've learned about the fundamental resources for shaping your life and taking control of it.

You've considered your horse and have a good understanding of what makes him tick. Now let's look at the specific tools needed to become a good rider. The first and most important step is to understand...

Chapter 7

RIDING SMARTER

Do what you can with what you have.
—Theodore Roosevelt

You now have all the tools you need to direct yourself. But you may not have the technical information needed to assist your progress. Riding a horse is really easy—ask any kid with a pony! But understanding how to get the absolute best from your horse—how to help him to reach his potential—needs knowledge.

Read, watch videos, listen to experts, observe the top riders and then take what you need and what makes sense to you. Remember there is often more than one right way to do something—some take longer than others and some are ineffective.

Every horseperson believes that what he is doing is the best way and, for him, it possibly is. The horseman who says, "I've been working with horses all my life," sounds very impressive, but it could mean he has been doing *wrong* things all his life! The instructor who is said to be the best may not know how to teach, or he may just be a good self-promoter. The beginner who flinches when she sees a horse being hit should trust her instincts. The smartest rider will base his decisions on logic and sound reasoning; it follows that the more knowledge you have, the better decisions you will make.

First of all, you need to know the best way to learn because you will never stop learning as long as you are involved with horses. Traditional methods of learning are not good enough for today—there are much more effective ways to learn than those used last century. Then you have to understand what it is that everyone talks about but no one can define: The Basics. We need to know about The Basics, so we can control and influence the horse successfully.

Finally you must know how to train your horse in the most effective way so there is always achievement and progress, never making a mistake and then losing time fixing it. Advanced training methods ensure rapid progression without sacrificing quality.

Getting from Klutz to Competent

Using a skill involves the ability to coordinate muscular contractions so that some deliberate change is brought about. It is a consequence of training and practice. Without training, the performance of a skill is impossible. It is different from a habit—a skill is adaptable and flexible.

There is no essential difference between what we call a genius and everybody else, except that the genius finds the correct method of organizing himself—sometimes by fortunate circumstances, but more often by searching for it. Once the best method is found, many can do as well and often better than the originator of the method. Many people fail to recognize the true cause of their inability or failure—it is very often not lack of ability, but improper use of self.

The expert rider produces only those movements that are wanted—this is what riding skill is. In the learning stage there are a lot of unwanted movements which are usually gross and use more effort than is necessary. The essential concept in learning to ride is to be able to recognize these unwanted movements and discard them.

The incompetent rider produces so much unnecessary, and often contradictory, action that the intended act is accompanied by an overwhelming sense of resistance, which inclines her to believe that the act is difficult. It is not the act itself that is hard—it is the discipline of eliminating unnecessary movements. To become competent at riding we need to learn to distinguish between essential, efficient movements and obstructive, inept ones.

In any coordinated and well-learned action we can identify certain features. It doesn't matter if we are sawing wood or chopping up carrots, the expert will always make it look easy, because there will be:

- **Absence of effort**—no wasted movement, the action looks easy.

- **Flexibility**—in a state of untension it is possible to be flexible and supple, to change our actions easily.

- **Breathing**—the experts are able to breathe normally because they are untense.

Bearing these things in mind, it becomes apparent that part of being a competent rider consists of being relaxed enough so there is no wasted movement, no imbalance and no tension.

Learning a Skill

When we go through the process of learning a new skill, activity or movement, we normally go through a series of recognizable stages. At the beginning, we are very left-brained and therefore need left brain type of instruction:

♦ We need verbal instruction.

♦ We can only handle small bits of information at one time.

♦ We have to consciously control our movements.

♦ We would like to be able to see what the action looks like.

♦ We have poor detection of errors.

As we become more skilled, we utilize right brain concepts more and more:

♦ We begin to be able to feel if it is right.

♦ We can approach the action as a whole instead of many little pieces.

♦ Our concern is more on the quality rather than the components of the movement.

♦ We can quickly and accurately detect any errors we make and usually fix them.

♦ Although we still need "eyes on the ground," we don't need such close instruction.

♦ We can now take much more responsibility for ourselves and the horse.

It is important for the rider to be aware of which side of the brain is being dominant. If the learning stage has gone past left-brain dominance, for example, the rider should consciously start to let go of the left-brain activity and allow right-brain functions to guide the body.

Being physically relaxed and using our minds constructively are two important parts of riding smarter. The third vital component is ....

Chapter 8
LEARNING BETTER AND FASTER

Thinking is the hardest work there is, which is probably why so few engage in it.

How Do We Learn?

Knowing how people learn is a big step toward learning faster and more effectively. The traditional methods of teaching riding have little connection with the modern scientific techniques which are based on recognized learning theory.

Understanding
Many instruction methods rely on an authoritarian approach from the instructor, with the student accepting without question what she is commanded to do. Often students aren't even allowed to talk during a lesson.

This old-fashioned approach is in total contradiction to effective learning. The rider should be encouraged to give feedback and to participate in the process. The instructor should provide reasons for what she requires.

The more the rider understands, the quicker she will learn. *Understanding* is absorbed by the right brain and remains available, whereas *commands* are handled by the left brain, which often has a problem remembering them. Therefore, when the rider has been told and shown what to do, she should then be allowed time to absorb this information.

Participation

The best way to learn anything is to *do it*—to be involved physically and mentally. In the educational field, it has been proven that participative learning is the most effective means of learning. It has been found that this is also the case when teaching riding.

Once the rider has mentally absorbed the new information, she then needs to physically do it—this lets the right brain and the muscles remember what it is all about.

Repetition

This can be a good learning tool (for people). We need to revise and review things a lot more than horses do. It seems that once they have the idea, they don't forget it. People, on the other hand, tend to forget more than 50 percent of new information if it's not revisited within 24 hours.

Visualization

After a workout or a lesson, when you are at home, you should mentally revise (visualize) what you have done. Your subconscious is not good at discerning between what is real and what you imagine. So if you see pictures of yourself doing something, the subconscious accepts that they are real and, in this way, learning can be achieved much quicker and easier.

Experiments have shown that when a rider *visualizes* an action a number of times (even without riding during that time), the action is significantly improved the next time it is attempted.

Physical repetition combined with visualization (mental training) provide the ideal conditions for fast learning.

Conditions For Effective Learning (ESI - Easy, Structured, Interesting)

In order to ensure effective learning, the lessons must be *easy*, there must be *structure* and the content must be *interesting*.

Easy

For successful learning we must proceed at our own rate. It must be pleasurable and not difficult.

In order for learning to be easy, it must be done in small steps. If there are a lot of small steps and each one is easy, the movement will be learned and it will be effortless. The same reasoning applies to the horse—if we make it easy for the horse to learn something (that is, break it down into small steps), we won't take risks, creating problems that then have to be rectified and wasting time.

Structured

In order to achieve peak performance, we have to do a lot of thinking. Most of this thinking should be done ahead of time. We should think about our goals and how to achieve them. We should also think a lot about what we are going to do when we ride.

Once we have decided what we are going to work on during the day's session, we then have to think how we are going to do it—how to break it down into small chunks, how to avoid mistakes, how to avoid resistances.

Every time we ride we must warm up the horse first and cool him down last. There must be a structure—a routine, for warming up—which creates the place from which learning can most effectively be done.

Interesting

If we have no interest in something, then trying to learn about that something becomes a chore, we are slow to learn and we don't remember a lot of what we thought we learned. If the work is boring with little variety and much repetition, not a lot will be learned. However, when we are motivated, we will learn very quickly and very well.

Don't always ride in the same arena or always in circles. Sometimes riding on the trails or jumping over logs or going for a canter can be the best thing for you and your horse. There should always be some challenge.

Aim for excellence, not perfection

The paradox of perfection: by expecting perfection in yourself you are making a huge mistake. Perfection may be necessary in certain areas of life, such as a computer programming or watchmaking but, in general, especially in riding, it isn't possible.

Aiming for perfection hinders effectiveness and wastes time and energy. It also provides a good excuse for lack of progress. It can actually keep you from achieving your important goals. Many perfectionists are frustrated doers who are afraid to make mistakes. Perfection means "no further improvement is possible." If you were a golfer would you stay on the first hole until you achieved a hole in one?

The Basics: Why Didn't Anyone Ever Tell Me?

Not only is there a real need for a definition of *the basics*, there is also a requirement that any smart rider knows and understands them so well that they are part of the rider/horse combination and utilized without even thinking about them.

Essentially, the only things we can teach the horse are our signals for stop, go, turn and yield. Everything else is developed from these. **Stop** includes halt, half halt and rein back; **go** includes walk, trot and canter, transitions and lengthenings; **turn** includes circles, serpentines and corners, and **yield** refers to sideways (lateral) work.

It is vital to have these key basics as second nature to both horse and rider, always achieved without force.

The Basics of Good Riding

Balance/Position

As riders, we have a choice of two ways of staying on the horse—we can hang on with our legs and hands (gripping) or we can be in equilibrium (balanced). These are two extremes of a continuum and most of us will use some degree of each at various times. The smartest riders will always be balanced—not only is this more comfortable, but also safer. If the rider is gripping, he is going to become unstable sooner or later. When the rider is balanced and untense, he is in a secure position.

Balance is achieved by sitting on the two seat bones in an untense way with your legs totally relaxed and loose, hanging down naturally and looking long. When they are this way, they act as an anchor, weighting you down into the saddle. As soon as you tense your inner thighs, they will shorten and push you upward and out of the saddle. The lower leg only is used to give aids to the horse.

Balance of the upper body is also important—it is not possible to be truly balanced unless the upper body is vertical and therefore in line with the horse's center of gravity. If the rider leans backward, he will have to compensate by either hanging onto the reins, or tensing muscles. The head is part of the upper body and should be balanced on the neck, not with the chin and neck pushed forwards. Again, deviation from balance indicates tension and often this comes as a result of concentration and/or determination.

Stillness

When we are balanced on our seat bones, we then have to be still—any unnecessary movements will cause equal and opposite reactions. The upper body needs to be untense, especially in the lower back. This is the optimum place to absorb the movement of the horse, as the spine there is slightly curved and able to straighten or curve more, as the situation demands.

Stillness is a strange concept—to be still and quiet on a horse requires the rider to have a very mobile pelvic area, which is always moving in order to accommodate the movement of the horse. If the lower back is unyielding, the movement cannot be absorbed there and travels upward until it finds the neck, which is quite mobile. As the neck absorbs the movement, the head bobs up and down, causing the rider to appear clumsy and ungainly.

The pelvis moves backward and forward while the rest of the body remains still.

Hands

In order for the hands to be still, the *elbows* need to be loose and mobile. Our hands must be still, because every time we move them, we move the bit in the horse's mouth. This either gives a signal to the horse and/or causes him pain. When we cause pain in the horse's mouth, he will react in some way (unless he has become very hard in the mouth as a defense against being hurt). He may open his mouth, jerk his head up or bring his head closer to his chest to get away from the pressure/pain.

Sometimes when riders don't want a horse to open his mouth they will adjust the noseband very tightly or add a flash noseband, which prevents this from happening. Unfortunately this is only treating the effect, not the cause and tends to make the problem worse. Because the noseband inhibits the jaw muscles, the tension from them will be spread through the horse's head and neck muscles, along the back and down the legs, making the whole horse resistant. The horse may also react by resisting, becoming aggressive, swishing his tail, keeping his ears back, snatching the reins, bucking, etc. The possibilities are many and unpleasant.

Far better to avoid these unwanted reactions by training the horse kindly so he doesn't need to protect himself from the rider. It has been found that releasing or taking off the noseband (particularly the lower part of a cavesson) drastically improves the behavior of the horse. Another reason for dispensing with a dropped noseband is that when used, it deadens the communication from the horse's mouth to the hands of the rider.

The Basic Movements

It doesn't matter if you are a dressage rider, show jumper, endurance rider, pleasure rider, or western rider, your horse should be able to do all of the following basic movements. If not, then you won't be able to get the best from your horse when it is needed in competition. Even riders that only go for pleasure rides or trail rides will benefit if their horses had these basic movements.

All performance horses should be able to do 20-meter circles, straight lines, serpentines, figure eights and leg yields. They should halt and perform transitions as soon as those aids are given.

The Technology of Training

These days training a horse is much more scientific than previously because we have much more information to work with and advanced equipment that can measure things we never could before.
The aims for scientific training are

♦ the horse responds immediately to our request,
♦ force is never used,
♦ the horse enjoys the work,
♦ the horse learns fast, i.e. after three repetitions,
♦ the horse understands verbal and physical signals,
♦ the horse should maintain his attention on us.

In scientific training, the principles of "Operant Conditioning" are used, as developed by Skinner, Hull, Spence, etc.

Operant Conditioning

This is the behavioral learning process that involves deliberate actions. *Operant* = active (deliberate actions), *Conditioning* = learning: **learning through deliberate actions**.
Operant conditioning is a type of learning in which behaviors are altered by the consequences which follow them. When a horse behaves in a particular way and the consequences of that behavior are in some ways reinforcing (rewarding) to him, he is likely to repeat that behavior. The term *operant* is used because the horse operates on the environment by learning to make a response that brings about a reward. This is sometimes referred to as "trial and error" training—that is, the horse is involved in the process by thinking and trying different behaviors and knowing when he has succeeded by gaining a reward. This is different from "Classical Conditioning," where the responses are instinctive, with no thought involved.

146

Reinforcement

Critical to operant conditioning is the concept of reinforcement (reward)—the strengthening of a new response by its repeated association with a stimulus/reward. When the horse responds with a behavior that is close to what the trainer wants, the trainer delivers a reward (positive reinforcer). For example, if the horse holds his leg up and a reward follows, the behavior of holding up his leg is likely to repeat under the same conditions.

Primary reinforcers (PR) are food and pain—these both have a very powerful effect on the horse. Because horses want to avoid pain and want to approach food and because inflicting pain will create an undesirable response, scientific training uses only reward, not punishment.

Secondary reinforcers (SR) such as voice and touch are not as strong as primary reinforcers. They will also have an effect on the horse, but not the intense motivational one that a primary reinforcer has. However, if the secondary reinforcer is linked to the primary reinforcer, the horse will then give it the same response as he originally gave the primary reinforcer.

For example, if we link food (PR) with a distinctive sound (SR), the horse will quickly learn to respond to the sound itself in the same way he responds to food.

In order to maintain its strong effect the secondary reinforcer needs to be fortified from time to time with the primary reinforcer or the response will diminish. So once the horse responds to the distinctive sound, give food with the sound every now and then to maintain the strength of the response.

Rewards

Psychologists often define reward (reinforcement) as *some change in the environment which increases the likelihood of the behavior being repeated.*

147

When training horses, food is often the strongest reward. This food can be carrots, apples, pellets, sugar cubes, or breakfast cereal such as Fruit Loops or Nutrigrain. It is important to remember that when training horses, the trainer needs to have both hands free; in other words, it can be very difficult to hold food in one hand while you are lunging the horse or doing in-hand training with a whip in one hand and a lunge line in the other. Cereals or small pieces of carrot or apple can be kept in a waist bag or a pocket; a whole carrot can be tucked into the waistband of your jodhpurs

The amount of reward given is relevant in this kind of training: one small treat such as one Fruit Loop, is sufficient for an appropriate response—the horse will appreciate it, even if it is very small. A larger treat (e.g. a handful of Fruit Loops) tells the horse he has done something really great.

Rewards should be given only when and if a behavior has been asked for and then occurs. So if the horse, after having learned that he will get a treat when he holds up his leg, then proceeds to hold up his leg every time he is near you, he should be ignored, because you didn't ask for that behavior. Your objective is to have the horse respond to your request, whether it is verbal or physical, not to perform tricks.

Rewards must never be used as bribes. Bribing means that treats are usually offered after the horse has been resisting. Thus, the reward may reinforce resistance in the future rather than doing the task without being reminded. Rewards should be given only after the desired behavior has occurred.

The reward must be immediate so it can be associated with the specific behavior of the horse. The trainer must wait for (or manipulate) the desired response.

With scientific training we set things up so the horse assumes an active role in the learning situation. The learning is not just something that happens arbitrarily. We want the training to be under our control for it to be effective, so we can teach and know that the horse has learned the lesson.

Fractional Goal Response

These are anticipatory responses that are partial components of the complete goal response (Hull, 1930; Spence, 1956, 1960). These incomplete responses might be chewing, looking, lifting a foot, or any other sort of response that would not interfere with the main task. They provide the horse with a kind of symbolic representation of the goal object. In effect, the fractional stimulus-response mechanism provides a means by which the horse, through conditioning, can come to think ahead and to anticipate possible rewards.

This is a very potent tool to use with the horse, as it enables us to train him to look forward to his time in a training session with us and to be using his brain whenever he is in our company.

Side Effects of Learning

Dr. Cecelia Pollock of Lehman College in New York has stated that learning creates brain capacity, which implies that the more a horse learns, the more intelligent he becomes. Electrical brain stimulation produces effects characteristic of reinforcement. This brings up the possibility that learning (brain stimulation) might be its own reinforcer, something that has been observed when training horses. It is possible that as learning stimulates the brain it may release endorphins, which are chemicals that make the horse feel good.

Timing

For an association to be made between the response and the reward, the reward must be made within one second of the response. If the timing is longer, the effect of the reward is diminished, confused or lost.

Intermittent or partial reinforcement is an important principle in operant conditioning. This happens after the horse has understood the lesson; the food reward is then only given intermittently, instead of every time the action is performed. This ensures that the horse's brain stays involved and also enables us to reinforce him verbally when he is too far away to give food.

If conditioning trials are spaced over fairly long intervals, the animal will learn to make the correct response more efficiently than if the trials are bunched together. Massed trials lead to a rapid buildup of fatigue which will inhibit learning. Spacing the trials allows fatigue to dissipate between each trial and lead to more efficient learning.

B.F. Skinner was the psychologist who is credited with the concept of operant conditioning. In 1938 he showed that learning takes place after the first three correct responses. He also found that

♦ increased strength of response means that increased learning is taking place, and

♦ the biggest additions to response strength occur early in learning, then drop off.

Food

Food is a primary stimulus, like fear, pain, sex, light, and freedom, which is the reason psychologists use it in many of their experiments with animals. Deliberate behavior is either to avoid (pain) or to approach (food/pleasure). Food is a better stimulus because of the pleasure factor—it doesn't extinguish easily. If pain is repeated, the horse will often switch it off and pain ceases to be a stimulus.

Some psychologists oppose rewards with humans because they emphasize the controlling or superior position of the rewarder and the dependent, inferior position of the rewardee. However, when training horses, it is beneficial for the trainer to be regarded as superior.

C.L. Hull found in 1952 that sucrose seems to have an innate taste appeal for animals as well as people. Giving horses sweet food is acceptable and doesn't rot their teeth.

Auditory Signals

Auditory signals—sounds—are secondary reinforcers. They are not as powerful or motivational as primary reinforcers.

An auditory signal can be a whistle, a noise made with a mechanical clicker, *brrrr* as used in Europe, or a cluck, made with the tongue on the roof of the mouth. The sound *aaah* can also be used as a calming aid for the horse.

These signals are used effectively as *bridging cues*—something that associates the primary reinforcer (e.g., food) with the correct behavior. They can often (when learned) take the place of the primary reinforcers, especially when it's not possible to give the horse food because you might be mounted, lunging or too far away to deliver it within the time frame of one second.

When training a horse it is important that the sound you make to signify, *Yes, that was right*, is distinctive, short, immediate and able to be given orally (because we need both hands to be free). This gives us choices such as whistle, *brrr* or a cluck, etc. The glottal cluck sound is usually the easiest one to make and the horse gets to recognize it very quickly (i.e., after three associations with a food reward). When the action has been asked for and given, the bridge signal (cluck) should be given followed by the the food reward.

Although words and phrases are also auditory signals, it's unlikely that they will increase the likelihood of the behavior being repeated and so they can't really be regarded as reinforcers. They are imprecise because they take a relatively long time to complete (remember the one second time frame) and during that time the horse could have done two or three other actions, making it impossible for him to understand which one was the right one.

Also, words and phrases are often used in many different situations, not only for training, again creating an unclear communication. When training more complex behavior we need to reinforce any indication of the desired behavior and this has to be done instantly—are clumsy and ineffectual in these situations.

The short, distinctive sound marks the exact time and behavior. The longer words are useful as encouragement and to indicate general satisfaction with the overall situation. For example, "What you are doing now is good" is different from, "What you did at that exact time was right."

Tactile Signals

These are anything that involves touch such as stroking the horse, tapping with a whip, scratching, or massage. Like auditory signals, tactile signals are also secondary reinforcers—the horse usually likes the pleasant ones, but they have only a minor role in a training situation.

There are, of course, other tactile signals that are unpleasant, such as patting the forehead, whacking the neck, whipping or hitting. These are destructive actions and don't even function as stimuli for the horse to avoid a particular behavior.

Chunking Down

This is a skill that is essential for the effective, scientific training of the horse. Most actions can be broken down into many parts and then it is possible to mentally arrange those parts in order of difficulty. The scientific trainer will then teach the easiest parts first and when they are understood, move on to the next parts. For example, let's consider teaching the horse to lift a specified leg and hold it up on your verbal command "foot." Chunking down this action we would get these parts:

1. Physically lifting the foot at the same time as we say "foot" (cluck, give treat).
2. Say "foot" and tap the foot or fetlock (cluck-treat). Only reward if the horse holds the foot up, not if he just lifts and drops it.
3. Say "foot" and touch the upper part of the leg (cluck-treat).
4. Say "foot" and point at the required leg (cluck-treat).
5. Only give the treat intermittently once the action is learned.
6. Don't cluck or treat if the action is offered without being asked for.

Notice that reinforcement is given at every stage of the process, not just when the whole action has been done correctly.

Starting Scientific Training

To train an animal, it is often helpful to lead the animal through a behavior in small steps. We can do this by using our hand. (When the behavior takes place farther away, we use a whip, which is simply an extension of our arm).

The first thing we want to achieve is to get the horse to touch our hand when we say, "touch." Of course he has no idea of what we want, so we probably will have to help him to understand by touching his nose with our hand, then rewarding him with food (from the other hand), then "cluck." You don't want to hold out the hand with food in it because then the horse will smell the food and he won't learn the "touch" lesson.

Very quickly the horse will start touching your hand with his nose—then you should move your hand further away, up, down, etc., and each time he touches it he should be rewarded. When he understands this game, you should only reward with food intermittently, but always with the "cluck" to reinforce.

It is a short step from touching your hand to touching the end of a stick or a whip. This is a very useful behavior to have, as you can stretch his neck to each side and down between his legs with it. It also teaches the horse not to be afraid of the whip.

Training a Complex Behavior

Shaping

Most behaviors cannot be learned all at once are developed in steps. This step-by-step learning process is called shaping.

Think of learning to ride a bicycle. Most of us started on a tricycle, went on to riding a two-wheeler with training wheels and eventually mastered a larger bicycle, maybe even one with multiple speeds. Each one of these little steps toward the final goal of riding a bicycle is reinforcing. This step-by-step learning process is an example of shaping.

By reinforcing small steps, we can train an animal to perform complex behaviors. The animal is first reinforced for a natural movement that somewhat resembles the desired trained behavior. We reinforce the animal for each step toward the final goal of the finished behavior.

Unwanted Behavior

If you request a particular behavior and the animal does not respond, or the animal responds with undesired behavior, remain motionless and silent for three seconds.

After those three seconds, training resumes. We never force a situation and we never punish an animal.

Unacceptable Behavior

Think *reprimand*, not *punish*. If a horse bites or kicks you, you should reprimand him, just as the herd leader would. This could be verbal (e.g. shouting) or physical (slap). Either way, the reprimand must be a single action, not repeated or continuous and occurring within half a second of the offense.

Accelerated Learning

There are very marked similarities between scientific training and "accelerated learning" for humans. Accelerated learning operates on a sub-conscious level, works on a relaxed and receptive state of mind and presents information in new ways that actively involve both hemispheres of the brain. A high proportion of learning takes place at a subconscious level, so the student is presented with new material in such a way that it is absorbed by both the conscious and subconscious mind.

The First Aims of Training

When we train a horse we want him to have three qualities—**calm, attentive** and **forward**. These three things are not only our aims for the horse, but they also are guides to the sequence of every training session.

When we first start riding the horse we have to ensure that he is calm before we attempt to do anything with him. Then we want him to give us his attention so we can communicate with his brain and also get immediate responses. And, finally, we ask the horse to go forward—straight and with impulsion, no resistances.

Calm

Horses, like humans, are incapable of learning if they are tense. Physical tension spreads to the brain and when the brain is tense it blocks the absorption of information. So we have to take as long as it takes to ensure that the horse is relaxed mentally and physically before we try to school him.

If we want the best from our horse, it makes sense to treat him well and to develop the attitude in him that will make our job easier. This attitude is one of being aware of what the rider is asking and of responding immediately. As a rider, you are mainly responsible for your horse's attitude. If we are nice to our horses, they will be more inclined to listen to us and to cooperate. If we hurt or abuse them, we will create a hostile attitude. When this happens, the solution usually involves some kind of force. Unfortunately, for most riders and horses this then becomes a vicious circle, starting with the rider's hands:

pain(rider) ➡**resistance**(horse) ➡**force**(rider) ➡**hostility** (horse).

One of the main aims of training a horse is to be able to communicate effectively—to encourage him to do what we want him to do. This is in contrast to the use of gadgets such as martingales, draw reins, chambons, severe bits—anything that acts by force on the horse's head— that are designed to prevent the horse from doing what we don't want it to do.

Occasionally, when retraining a horse who has bad habits, gadgets have a place, but only a temporary one. They should only be used to achieve a specific aim and then be put away.

The smart rider will therefore train the horse in such a way so he doesn't develop habits that have to then be prevented by some kind of force. We want the horse to respond to our aids and the more immediate the response is, the better; we aim not to make mistakes that have to then be fixed, thus wasting time.

Attentive

If your horse is attentive to you, this will be for one of two reasons—either he wants to pay attention and concentrate because he enjoys the rewards that accompany this attitude, or he is afraid not to be, because of painful repercussions. The rewards are not necessarily from the rider. Horses, like us, get a buzz from achieving something and they feel good after gymnastic exercise. If we can take advantage of this, then again, we will be able to avoid using force.

We need the horse to be attentive to our aids and not looking at other horses, shying at plastic bags, etc. If the horse is attentive he cannot be distracted; he is concentrating and using his energy in an efficient and cooperative way. When he is in this state, we will be more likely to obtain immediate responsiveness.

When the horse gives us his attention, he is then ready to work and learn. The operative word here is "give"—attention isn't something we can *take* from the horse. We can only ask for it. So we have to be very thoughtful in the way we go about this. We must be patient and encouraging, leading the horse gradually from work on a loose rein into more contact, more bending and more impulsion. If we jump on and immediately start demanding work that requires muscular and/or mental effort, we will create resistances of some kind and lose attentiveness. Then we say the horse is not in a good mood or he is having a bad day. These things are probably true, but the cause is the rider, not the horse.

We can lose a horse's attention for a number of reasons—boredom, pain, tiredness, hunger, distractions, etc. Often when we give the horse a rest, his attention will wander as well. When we have lost the horse's attentive-

157

ness, we can't *make* him concentrate again. We have to *coax* him back to the state we want. This is best done by using the same techniques we employed when warming up—working on a loose rein, changes of direction, transitions, etc. It may take five minutes, but it is worth the time to maintain a calm attitude and to be able to continue the work already started.

There is a school of thought that never lets the rider rest during a schooling session because then the horse will stop concentrating and won't come back on the bit again. This is a sad admission of incompetence from these instructors.

Forward

Horses must go forward—this is the way they are built and the way they function best. Going forward means moving with impulsion. Even when doing lateral work, they are still going forward, never sideways only. Even when doing rein back, the *attitude* of the horse is still "forward" and he should go forward immediately after the rein back is finished.

The horse can't go *properly* forward unless he is *straight*—any crookedness impedes the flow of energy through the horse, affecting the forwardness. When the horse is going properly forward he is straight. He is tracking up, well balanced, with rhythmical, regular paces.

To achieve straightness, the horse must be supple longitudinally and laterally. The suppling exercises in turn create strength.

Often the *rider* will cause the horse to become crooked by tilting the horse's head, bending his neck, etc.. The horse, being willing and cooperative, merely does what the rider is telling it to do. If the rider wants the neck bent, it bends.

When there is pain associated with the rider's demands, the horse will resist—he blocks the movement, stops the flow of energy and compromises the forwardness of the movement. Most resistances are the result of the rider's lack of sensitivity.

Sometimes we ask the horse to do work that he isn't physically strong enough to do. The only way he can cope is to become crooked in some way. Most horses are one-sided—they find it easier to do things on one side than on the other. The smart rider will try and even up this one-sidedness and make the horse straight, thus achieving better responsiveness and attentiveness. You can achieve this by performing consistent gymnastic work evenly in both directions so the horse becomes strong and supple.

The Basic Techniques

Pressure

One of the main aims of a rider is to have the horse respond *immediately* to an aid he has been given. Horses tend to move away from brief pressure, but lean into consistent pressure. Initially the pressure from our legs means "go" and will probably not be very subtle—more often a "kick." This will usually be refined into a more subtle and kinder squeeze.

Because the horse moves away from momentary pressure (a brief squeeze) and because the horse is built to move forward, when we squeeze with *both* legs, the only way the horse can go is forward.

If we squeeze with one leg, we expect the part of the horse receiving pressure to move away.

Therefore, if we apply pressure at the girth, the horse will bend away (very slightly) from that point. And if we apply pressure just behind the girth, the hindquarters will move away. However, if we move our leg backward more than about the length of our foot, the aid loses its effectiveness and our weight is displaced to the outside.

So our inside leg must always be on the horse's girth and our outside leg always just slightly behind the girth.

The amount of pressure we apply with either or both legs then dictates what the horse will do.

Ideally our legs and hands should always be in contact with the horse—legs always touching the horse, hands in contact through straight reins from the rider's elbow to the bit (except when on a long or loose rein). The reason for this is so that we don't surprise or hurt the horse, with a bang in the mouth or by a leg thumping on and off. Also, when we are in constant contact we are able to give subtle, precise aids, causing the least possible interference to the horse.

Half Halts

As a basic technique, the half halt is used mainly to get the horse's attention. It's a way of saying, "Hey!" without speaking.

There are many different kinds of half halts, ranging from the very simple and crude tug on the reins, to the subtle and very effective seat, legs and hand aid used by many advanced riders. The most effective simple half halt is a taking and giving of the outside rein while the inside rein is held still. And the important thing to remember is that it is the *release* of the half halt that has the effect. In other words, make the taking part very brief and release immediately.

The basic half halt is also used to signal the horse to slow down or stop. If he is going too fast, a rider's natural reaction is to pull on the reins. This is counter-productive for two reasons:

♦ if the horse is bolting he won't even feel it.

♦ if he is just exuberant, your pulling on the reins will induce him either to pull against you so he won't get hurt or to run faster in order to escape the pain.

So what is the solution? In the case of the bolter, grab one rein close to the bit and physically turn the horse into a tight circle. With the running horse, use half halts—each one being a small tug, but always giving immediately before the horse can pull against you. Sometimes the untrained horse won't respond immediately, in which case repeat the half halt—as many times as necessary to bring him back under control. But be patient and don't expect perfect results straight away. The half halt is a signal that is learned by the horse, not a guaranteed effect.

Diagonal Aids

Many times we create crookedness in the horse by pulling on the inside rein. This can happen either because we want him to turn or because we have an incorrect understanding of bend. Unfortunately, this often has the opposite effect—when we bend the neck and pull the head around, we unbalance the weight distribution in the front of the horse, making the horse fall on to his outside shoulder in order to compensate for the imbalance we have created. Contrary to popular belief, the horse doesn't always follow his head around but more often follows his shoulder. So when we make him throw his weight onto his shoulder, he has to go in that direction or he might fall over.

In order to avoid unbalancing the horse in front, we have to keep his neck straight. To achieve this, use increased contact on the outside rein while keeping the inside rein a bit shorter and still. And if we want the horse to turn, we have to bend his body so that his shoulders are facing the direction we want to go. To achieve this, use increased pressure from the inside leg.

This combination is referred to as *diagonal aids* (or inside leg to outside rein) and is one of the most effective techniques we have. It is also used for lateral work, to collect the horse and to bring him onto the bit.

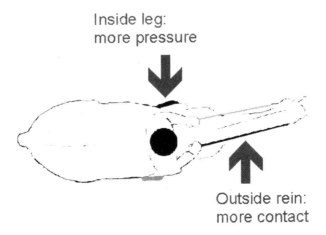

Inside leg:
more pressure

Outside rein:
more contact

Diagonal aids emphasize the inside leg and the outside rein.

Gymnastic work

In any equestrian activity where the horse is required to not only carry a load, but also to perform difficult physical exercise, gymnastic work must be a major focus of his training. Gymnastic means developing strength and agility.

To increase agility we must encourage the horse to contract and lengthen his body—bending in both directions, collecting and extending. To build strength we need to work the horse a little bit more than is comfortable for him each time we ride. If your horse is not very fit or muscled up, it is important to recognize signs of fatigue (resistance, shaking the head, etc.) during gymnastic work and give him a rest by walking on a loose rein, allowing the head and neck to stretch long and low.

Chapter 9
Training—Something To Look Forward To

To get a horse fully trained to the highest standard takes a long time, about three years.
—Franz Mairinger

To be effective, training must be methodical, thoughtful and enjoyable for you and the horse. It doesn't matter what we are doing with our horse—jumping, eventing, dressage, endurance or hacking, there are three things we must be ultimately aiming for. These are for the horse to be calm, attentive and forward. Therefore, all of the training of the horse must always be done with these things uppermost in our minds.

These goals are also our immediate aims and the structure of the process when working with green horses.

Conditioning the Dressage Horse

Physiological preparation of the dressage horse is often limited to training the required movements without utilizing an overall plan to insure the horse's fitness. There are three phases of the horse's fitness with which we should concern ourselves. These are: respiratory, suppling and strength training. Unlike other performance horses that are conditioned for speed or stamina, the dressage horse needs to develop strength and suppleness. The principles of interval training are utilized, as in any good training method and applied with strength and suppleness as outcomes. Respiratory fitness is the all-important limiting factor in getting any horse fit. This is one reason it is recommended to work the horse just a little bit more each time.

Distance work is not a real issue in this form of conditioning. However, it is important for the horse to be worked regularly on hard surfaces like roads or tracks in order to strengthen his tendons, ligaments and bones.

Dressage movements in themselves are designed to develop strength and suppleness, but it is important for the horse to be strong enough to carry out the movements being asked of him. Training is a progression, not just the achievement of a particular movement and then moving on to the next one. Therefore, dressage movements should be introduced in a specific sequence, not randomly chosen on the day. Dressage tests provide an excellent guide for this. The horse should always be stronger and more supple than is required for the movement being asked of him.

All the major systems (respiratory, cardio-vascular, musculo-skeletal) need to be developed, but it is especially important not to hinder the horse's respiration. Inhaling is the source of oxygen for muscles and energy and exhaling gets rid of carbon dioxide. If these two actions are not carried out and balanced, the other systems won't work as efficiently as they should. The most common ways of obstructing the flow of air are flexing the horse's head come close to his neck and lifting the neck so it approaches the vertical. Any forced head or neck positions will restrict the horse's capacity for air intake and exhalation. This inhibits the amount of oxygen that can get to the muscles and, as a result, the muscles tire easily, create a buildup of lactic acid, hurt during and after work and will not increase substantially in size and strength.

The following points should all be included when working out a training/conditioning program for the dressage horse.

Interval Training: hard work alternating with relaxation, intensity alternating with duration.

Progressive Loading: always ask more than you did last time.

Hill Work: a 10-percent incline requires 50 percent more effort than needed on a level surface—ideal for fast, safe conditioning if done with careful thought.

Occasional Speed Work: toughness, lung expansion and fun.

Road Work: develop muscles, strengthen bones, tendons and ligaments in the legs.

Bending: thoracic suppleness, strengthening of the hindquarters.

Transitions: balance, hindquarter strength, back and abdominal muscle development.

Lateral Work: shoulder suppleness, hindquarter strength and suppleness.

Collection: upward thrusting power, loading of the hindquarters, longitudinal shortening.

Extension: forward thrusting power, loading of the hindquarters, longitudinal elongation.

Muscle building is accomplished by the breakdown of tissue during hard work that the body restores during the next 24 hours. We need to allow adequate time for this repair to take place, therefore intense work should not be done on two consecutive days. If the horse is stabled, he should be ridden every day, but every second day should consist of very light work. Contrary to expectations, this actually conditions the horse faster than working him hard every day. If the horse is not stabled, he will get sufficient exercise outside and should be allowed to have every second day off, in order for his muscle tissue to restore.

All conditioning work needs to start minimally, gradually increasing in intensity and duration. The size of the 20-meter circle is knowledgeably chosen, as this diameter is one that will not put any physical strain on an unfit horse. Likewise, a 10-meter circle requires more bending ability and the 6-meter volte is the smallest bend we can ask for without the horse swinging out his hindquarters.

Similarly, when starting transition work, we begin with easy, between-gaits work: halt-walk, walk-trot, trot-walk, etc. Gradually add transitions in and out of the canter, while being aware that the horse needs to have a certain amount of strength to canter with a rider on his back. As strength increases, transitions within the gaits (collecting and lengthening) and over gaits (walk-canter, trot-halt, etc.) can be introduced.

Lateral work can be introduced quite early in the training program, starting with simple leg yielding and progressing to shoulder-fore, shoulder-in and travers as the horse builds strength, suppleness and understanding. As leg yielding isn't a gymnastic exercise, no muscling is required for it. Small amounts (three to four strides) of shoulder-in can be done on an unfit horse, but sustained lateral work requires—and develops—strength and suppleness.

Collecting and lengthening work, while being advanced movements, should not be started until after the horse has developed some strength and balance. Back muscles and gaskins should show some definition and bulk before any serious work of this nature is attempted.

As a general guide, if the horse is conditioned correctly

and worked every second day, within about six weeks he should be sufficiently muscled to handle any movements appearing in First Level tests. This is not suggesting that within six weeks your horse can compete in a First Level test; it's just a guide as to the kind of strength and suppling you could expect to see in that time frame.

As the horse is worked correctly, building strength and transferring weight onto the hindquarters, he will have to bring in the head and neck back to balance as the hindquarters become lower and the hind legs come further underneath the body. This is a natural biomechanical progression and must not be imposed by the rider trying to put the horse in a frame, or make him go on the bit.

To give a basic understanding to what is required of the horse in different situations, here are some guidelines. The horse's resting heart rate can range from 25 to 40 beats per minute (BPM). In extended walk the rate is around 62 BPM. Collected trot for most horse is 80–100 BPM, collected canter is 100–120, piaffe around 140. The heart rate increases in lateral movements, rein-back and all technically difficult movements. This is important to keep in mind because the repeated muscle movements that cause the increase in heart rate also causes lactic acid production in the muscles. Lactic acid buildup in the muscles affects the horse's coordination, thus his ability to perform. In any schooling session there should be many resting periods where the horse is encouraged to stretch and relax while walking—an exhausted horse should never be worked.

Riding cross-country, especially cantering cross-country is good cardiovascular, respiratory and muscular exercise for your horse. Keeping the horse outside where he is able to enjoy natural suppling and strengthening will also keep him fitter. It has been shown that stabled horses lose bone density and thus are more susceptible to injury.

Beginning Training

As stated previously, the three most important objectives when starting to work with your horse are, in order of priority, calm, attentive and forward. These must be achieved in every session before anything else is attempted. If you are working with a young horse, it might take several sessions before you have calmness—but you must have it before you can progress further. As the horse becomes calm, his attention will be directed more towards you and only then can you start teaching.

Calmness Must Come First

First we must ensure that the horse is calm—not tense or frightened. This is because we need to reach his brain and tension or fear will not allow this to happen. So we have to be very careful not to instill fear in the green horse and alternatively we must eliminate fear from the anxious horse that has been mistreated. The fear will usually be one of pain. Obviously in the early stages of training we must not hurt or frighten the horse at all. This means not scaring him when catching him or putting on new gear such as roller, saddlecloth, bridle. Also be careful when doing things such as tightening up the girth, mouthing, long-reining. When mounting, lunging and teaching leg aids, take each process step by step, rewarding the horse when he does what you want or persisting until he does what you want.

For example, don't teach a horse to lunge by scaring him away from the lunging whip. Instead, teach him to move forward when touched on the hind leg with the whip.

If the horse isn't hurt or frightened in the early stages of training, he will trust you and be willing to work more with you. He will regard you as the leader of the herd and try to please you. Then you will be able to achieve more and more, knowing that the horse *wants* to cooperate.

Attention is Always Essential

Only when the horse is calm can we then expect him to be attentive to us and what we are teaching him. And, when starting training, he can only give us his attention for about 10 minutes at a time. Therefore, little and often is a good guide. Three 10 minute sessions in a day will be much more productive than one half hour session. The horse remains interested in what is happening, gets rewarded many times and looks forward to the next session. He doesn't get bored, tense or irritated, losing concentration and then not doing what we ask, therefore not getting rewarded.

Because the horse is attentive, he will respond to our signals. The more attentive he is and the better trained, the quicker the response will be. Obviously it is undesirable to have a horse that responds five minutes after you have given the signal—we want the response to happen as soon as possible after the aid.

When the horse is attentive, he is interested and therefore learning. When he loses his concentration, he stops learning. So if we ask him to do many boring repetitions his brain turns off, he loses attention and he stops learning.

When a horse does something right and is rewarded, he knows what he has done. Repeating the same thing lots of times after that only results in wasting your time.

The Horse Must Go Forward

The first lessons should be about teaching the horse to go forward—on a lead, on command, walking and trotting, etc. When the horse is past this stage, forward is still a priority. Now forward means not only moving in the forward direction, but going with impulsion, being straight, balanced and regular.

Forward impulsion comes from the hind legs, but this can't be established if there is a brake in the mouth—hands must always *allow* the flow of energy.

169

All horses are born one-sided—this means they will bend more easily to one side than the other. The trainer's job is to create a muscularly balanced horse, able to bend equally on both sides. Only when this has occurred can the horse be straight. And only a straight horse can go forward correctly. "Forward" means having the hind legs equally loaded, giving identical support to the spine.

In order to make the horse "straight" (that is, with the same flexibility on both sides) we need to educate him to coordinate his movements by bending and circling on his stiff side. The limbs on both sides must be used with equal energy.

With the crooked horse, the hind feet don't follow in the tracks of the front feet. The horse also causes the rider to sit crookedly, with more weight on one side than the other, thus increasing the horse's crookedness.

Straightness also means that when the horse is bent, his whole body follows the arc of the circle, with the hindlimbs tracking the front limbs. This inflexion is created not by the inside rein, but by the rider's inside leg. If the horse's neck or head is flexed inward more than the rest of his body, the horse is not straight, he is unbalanced and the regularity of movement is upset.

Forward also means "without resistances." In German this is called *Durchlassigkeit* (pronounced derk-lass-ig-kite); the nearest equivalent in English is probably "permeability"—going through without obstruction. It is also often translated as "throughness." It applies to the mental as well as the physical aspect of the horse.

If the horse experiences pain in the mouth, he will not go forward. If he even has a *fear* of pain, he won't go forward consistently and unhesitatingly. So the horse needs to be able to trust that the rider isn't going to hurt him. If he places his head just in front of the vertical, he is at the same time exposing himself to the potential for the most pain from the rider's hands. Therefore we see many horses either with their heads up, or behind the vertical—both are evasions and are the direct result of insensitive hands.

If the rider is tactful and doesn't hurt the horse's mouth, the horse will eventually carry his head just in front of the vertical, without having to be forced into this position by the rider. He will also be confident enough to lengthen or collect his paces when asked, knowing that these requests do not mean pain in the mouth.

Dressage movements and exercises are all concerned with building up the muscles in the hindquarters in order to develop straightness and to recreate the balance that is lost when there is a person in the saddle.

Training Sessions

Performance horses are also just horses—they need work in order to build up muscles and learn things and they also need to have relaxing and different exercises such as pleasure rides, occasional jumping, etc.

It is often said that if we work the horse too much he will get sour or flat—this is because the work is usually repetitive, boring and nonrewarding. The smart rider will make the work interesting and motivating and intersperse work sessions with occasional fun times.

A training session should consist of:
1. warming up
2. schooling
3. cooling down

Depending on the age, fitness and experience of the horse, a work session can last for 30 minutes or two hours. The work should not be boring. Constantly going around in never-ending circles isn't interesting, so don't do it. But then how do we teach the horse to do circles? We don't. We teach him to respond to our aids. The *rider* is the one who needs to know how to ride a circle and that can be learned in two minutes.

Your work with the horse must be enjoyable for both you and your horse—something you both look forward to and to feel good about afterwards.

Find many opportunities to reward your horse, both by touching him and also by voice. Remember that it can also be very effective *not* to reward him—this is noticed and works much better than punishment or verbal abuse. Don't underestimate the intelligence of your horse—he notices things, learns fast and has pride in what he does well.

Every time you work your horse you need to achieve something. This not only guarantees progress, but helps enormously with motivation for both of you. In order to ensure that you achieve and not go backwards, you have to plan what you will do and make sure you don't make any mistakes. The way to not make mistakes is to take no risks, always progressing in small steps.

Warming Up

Warming up the horse achieves three things—it gets the blood flowing around the body faster, stretches the muscles and encourages the horse pay attention to you. Until these things happen, there isn't much point in doing any schooling.

Every time you warm up you should follow the sequence of the three principles mentioned before—calm, attentive and forward.

Warming up and schooling both work on the mental and physical aspects, with emotional stability underlying everything we do.

Calmness

Our first goal is to prepare the horse:
+ mentally to become ready to work and
+ physically to increase the rate of blood flow.

It is important at the beginning of a schooling session to just do some easy, loose-rein walk, rising trot and canter. This also makes a smooth link between the horse standing around doing nothing in a paddock or stable and the actual hard work of schooling and supporting the rider. The horse will be less inclined to resist when you start to ask for more gymnastic work.

Attentive

In the second phase of warming up we are aiming
*   mentally to get the horse's attention and
*   physically to bend the horse in each direction.

By bending the horse, with slightly more contact, we are stretching the muscles along the sides of the horse. By constantly changing direction, we will also gain his attention.

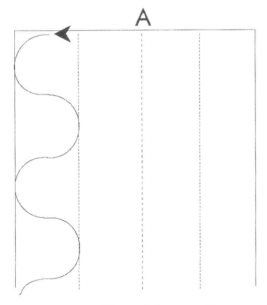

The mini-serpentine exercise

Bending work consists of walking and trotting circles, spirals, serpentines and corners. Because this bending work is primarily for the lateral muscles, we must ensure that it is the body we are bending and that the neck is kept straight.

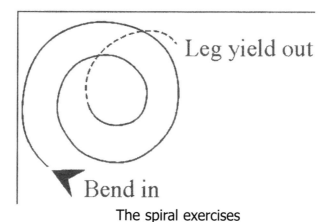

The spiral exercises

The figure eight exercise

Forwardness

In the third phase we want to
+ ensure that the horse is going freely forward,
+ keep the calmness and attention already gained, and
+ stretch and contract the body of the horse both laterally and longitudinally.

We must now retain the trust of the horse and be very careful not to create resistances through un-giving hands. This involves transitions—walk to trot to walk, trot to canter to trot, halt to rein-back to walk. Advanced flexing work involves transitions *inside* the gait—lengthenings to collection, etc.

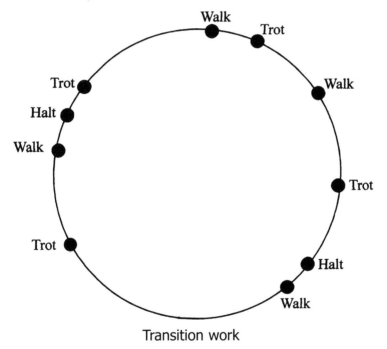

Transition work

When we work on lateral (sideways) movements, we combine bending and flexing—this is the best form of muscling, suppling and keeping the horse's attention.

It is just as important to keep the forwardness in lateral work as it is in all other work. If the horse seems to be stiffening at this point, the first thing to do is to loosen the reins and relax your hands and arms.

This warming up can take up to 15 minutes, reducing to about five to 10 minutes as you both become more proficient. Because you always follow the same routine, warming up and doing these exercises before a competition will help calm and focus the horse, as the work is familiar.

Teaching The Horse To Focus

If we are going to teach the horse something, we must have his attention or he won't learn. Therefore, getting the attention of the horse, or training him to focus, must be one of our aims when warming up.

We start with a structured, consistent warm-up routine; one which is done every time we ride. Use exercises you have thought about in advance and planned.

Even though you will be doing the same things every time we warm up, always ask for different things within those structured exercises. If you do repetitive, boring exercises, the horse will lose focus very quickly.

Be unpredictable—if you are doing mini-serpentines (from the long side to the quarter line only), sometimes do a complete small circle. If you are doing transitions, make them at different places in the arena between as well as within the gaits with halts and rein-backs. Keep them constantly changing.

Keeping the horse's attention means having his brain occupied on what you want.

What Are The Signs Of A Focused Horse?

♦ He stops looking around he is starting to focus on you.

- His head is approaching the vertical and softening at the poll with his ears coming back to you.

- He will give in the back, which will result in an easier ride for you.

- You will get a good response from subtle aids.

- You will get a more immediate response to your aids.

- Your horse may be slightly anticipating. Don't punish this but accept it as a sign of intense focus.

Schooling

The middle part of your work with the horse is the actual schooling—where you are teaching or refining things. This doesn't have to be very long—in fact, 10 to15 minutes is usually enough for actual work time, with another five minutes resting by walking around in the middle of the work if it's strenuous.

Small Steps: Make the work easy for your horse. Break down every new thing into its graduated components so that there are no surprises and no risks. You must be confident that you will succeed with each step.

Specific Issues: Teach only one thing at a time. This applies to both the horse and the rider. If the horse is learning to halt, teach him to halt—don't worry if his head isn't right; fix that after he has learned the halt lesson. If the rider's hands need adjustment, concentrate on them only—ignore anything else that is incorrect. You can always fix them later, one by one. To do this successfully you have to prioritize and select the most important area to work on first.

Reward and Rest: Make sure that your horse wants to keep working with you. Reward him both verbally and physically every time he makes an effort in the right direction. Don't wait until it is perfect. Rest him after every period of intense exercise.

Cooling Down

If you don't cool down your horse after working, you run the risk of his muscles getting cold quickly, before lactic acid buildup has time to dissipate. When lactic acid remains in the muscles, they get stiff and painful and can cause the horse to tie up.

Five minutes of walking around will usually cool him down. Check the large veins in his neck and body. If they were raised when you finished working, when they begin to subside the horse is returning to normal.

Problem Solving

There are many ways in which we can cause problems for our horses—rarely does the horse cause a problem for us.

When there is a problem, as a general rule, remember once again those three most important training principles: calm, attentive and forward. First—you must reestablish the calmness. Without this you can do nothing because the horse's brain will not work unless he is calm.

Second—get the horse's attention back. Go back to the place in the sequence where the horse was secure and gradually work forwards from there. Take him back until he is relaxed and can think again.

And third, go forward—but in small steps, waiting until the horse is confident before taking the next step. For example, if the horse stops dead in front of a puddle, don't try and make him go through it. Break down the challenge into smaller pieces: first just let him look at it; then circle around and back to the puddle a few times, getting closer each time; follow another horse through or dismount and let him follow you, one step at a time.

When there is a problem to be solved, be prepared to take as long as it takes. Don't rush and be patient. Focus on what the horse needs in order to overcome his problem, not what you want to be doing.

The next page offers a quite simplified, but often useful, table of problems and some possible reasons and solutions.

Problem	Possible Reason	Possible Solution
pulling	fear, pain, habit	half halts, soften rein aids
resistance	pain, tiredness	check gear, teeth, and movement of your hands
rearing	habit, fear	get a new horse or have an expert retrain him
crookedness	resistance, lack of fitness, stiffness	use more suppling exercises
lack of motivation	work not enjoyable	reward often, vary the sessions
unresponsiveness to aids	aids too strong or too long, horse inattentive	refine the aids
lack of focus	untrained	longer and better warming up

And now for something even more fun....

Chapter 10
COMPETING—
THE ULTIMATE
ADRENALINE HIT

Competition is as much process as goal.
—Harvey Ruben

If you manage them properly, competitions can really be fun. They also will help you prove to yourself that you are achieving things and reaching your goals.

You will never know how good you are until you compete. This is because competition conditions present the toughest you will ever encounter and until you ride under the hardest possible conditions, you will never know how you and your horse will handle them.

There are three benefits from competing, or performance riding:

       1. Learning
       2. Assessment
       3. Performance

Generally we focus on only one of these three benefits and miss out on the other two.

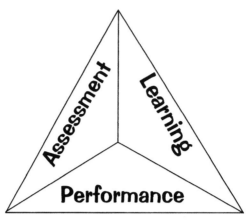

The Benefits of Competing

Enjoyment comes while working the horse, while competing and also after the competition. Some riders look only for the pleasure derived from winning and miss the joy of pure riding and learning new movements. Part of the learning process is the actual growth as a person that happens as you become a smarter rider—you have more self-esteem, more confidence, less ego problems, etc.

When an imbalance occurs, the benefits triangle tends to collapse. For example, when learning becomes the only goal, we tend to develop the "ivory tower syndrome": lots of knowledge but ineffective action and a lack of enjoyment. When performance is the only aim, learning is ignored. When assessment alone is the goal, the quality of riding can suffer and enjoyment is lost.

It isn't necessary to aim for total experience of all three things every day. Some days you may decide to ride just for fun; other days might be for learning a specific thing and others might be mainly for goal achievement. The particular goals should be set at least a week before you compete.

The way you conduct yourself when competing, whether you win or lose, shows the world what you are made of.

Overcoming "Show Nerves"

Some people get nervous days before a competition and can suffer greatly from this. Some of the symptoms are lack of appetite, irritability, moodiness, insomnia, lack of interest in riding and wanting to scratch from the show.

There are two main reasons for getting show nerves: being unprepared or placing too much importance on the event. The most important thing is to be prepared—in fact, be overprepared. Know the test, be confident jumping in excess of the height required, etc. Always compete at a level below the one you are currently working in.

Being prepared also involves having everything ready the day before: clean tack, inspect the trailer (check air pressure in all tires including the spare), check the car (fuel, oil, fluids, tire pressure), clean clothes, polish boots, wash the horse two days before and have him shod at least one week before, hitch the trailer, pack the horse's feed and water, plan the route, etc. Don't leave anything until the last minute. Aim to arrive an hour before you think you need to be there.

The other kind of nerves are the ones that hit you a little while before you actually enter the competition—you can't breathe, your legs get wobbly, you forget everything you worked on for the past two weeks. The solution here is first to *breathe* and second to *do something*—take some kind of physical action like warming up, checking gear, do some loosening exercises. Then decide to let go of all these distractions—just do it.

If the rider and/or the horse is green, nervous or excited, a good trick is to warm up twice. Do a small warm up for about 10 minutes, then rest for about an hour, then do your normal long warm up so that you will finish about five minutes before your classes.

Handling Competitions

The pursuit of victory leads to a deterioration in performance. If you go into a competition with the sole intention of winning, you are likely to be disappointed nine times out of 10. Many riders don't have the psychological makeup to successfully handle this scenario and consequently they suffer many disappointments, frustration and nerves.

In any sporting event, the competitor has very little control over the results. In equestrian competition, more than any other, we have even less control because there is another thinking, feeling being involved. We may have some measure of control over our horses, but when the unexpected occurs, anything can and does happen.

All riders go through predictably nervous reactions that can, if not managed properly, directly influence their performance on the day of competition. During this time the rider can go through a wide range of arousal fluctuations from extreme tension to extreme lethargy. Whenever she experiences arousal levels that differ significantly from her normal levels, she finds it increasingly difficult to concentrate and to think clearly and often becomes moody and irrational.

It is therefore useless to concentrate our efforts on *winning*, because we can't control that. It's much better to focus on things we can control, such as having the necessary knowledge, practicing, controlling our nerves and arriving on time. Fortunately, these are precisely the things that are necessary in order to have a chance of doing well. The rider who desperately wants to win and gets very uptight, arrives late and hasn't practiced much, is probably not going to win because of these factors, not because they are incompetent.

- Know the requirements of the event and visualize your dressage test or jumping course many times.

- Don't try and improve anything at the show or on the day before—invariably this makes things worse. If you are unsure of something, *visualize* it being done correctly.

- Be packed and ready to leave the day before the competition. Go to bed early and get enough sleep.

- Leave so that you arrive at least two hours before your first class and remember Murphy's Law: If anything can go wrong, it will.

- When you and your horse get settled in, warm up properly, allowing 10 minutes more than at home.

- Concentrate on your breathing just before you start, then visualize the first movement or jump.

If you want to win (and what competitor doesn't), you have to *not* think about winning. Concentrating on victory increases pressure, which increases tension and as soon as this happens, your riding will suffer. Concentrate instead on riding as well as you can.

While many other sports encourage an increase in arousal levels, riding demands coolness for success. So we have to do everything we can in order to create and maintain coolness.

- Consider that this event is only one part of a continuing process, not a "do or die" effort. Keep a long-term perspective and accept that what happens today isn't as important as it feels at the time.

- Realize that other competitors aren't nearly as interested in you as you might think.

- Have your own set of achievable goals, all of which are under your control.

- You are going out there to ride as well as you can.

Above all, remember that riding is something to be enjoyed. At the purest level riding can be a near-spiritual experience, with two minds and bodies functioning as one. At the other end of the scale it can be the best fun you ever had.

Both ends of the equestrian spectrum are worth all the hard work, frustrations and dedication that are integral parts of the whole experience.